BLACKSHIRTS AND REDS

BOOKS BY MICHAEL PARENTI

Contrary Notions (2007)

Superpatriotism (2004)

The Assassination of Julius Caesar (2003)

The Terrorism Trap: September 11 and Beyond (2002)

To Kill a Nation: The Attack on Yugoslavia (2001)

Democracy for the Few (1974, 1977, 1980, 1983, 1988, 1995, 2001)

History as Mystery (1999)

America Besieged (1998)

Blackshirts and Reds: Rational Fascism and the Overthrow of Communism (1997)

Dirty Truths (1996)

Against Empire (1995)

Land of Idols: Political Mythology in America (1994)

Inventing Reality: The Politics of News Media (1986, 1993)

Make-Believe Media: The Politics of Entertainment (1992)

The Sword and the Dollar (1989)

Power and the Powerless (1978)

Ethnic and Political Attitudes (1975)

Trends and Tragedies in American Foreign Policy (1971)

The Anti-Communist Impulse (1969)

BLACKSHIRTS AND REDS

Rational Fascism and the Overthrow of Communism

MICHAEL PARENTI

CITY LIGHTS BOOKS
San Francisco

Cover design: Nigel French
Book design: Nancy J. Peters
Typography: Harvest Graphics

Library of Congress Cataloging-in-Publication Data

Parenti, Michael, 1933–
    Blackshirts and reds : rational fascism and the overthrow of
communism / Michael Parenti.
        p.   cm.
    ISBN 0-87288-330-1 (hc). — ISBN 0-87286-329-8 (pbk.)
    1. Communism.   2. Post-communism.   3. Fascism.
4. Capitalism.   5. Free enterprise.   6. Anti-communist movements.
7. Revolutions.
I. Title.
HX44.5.P35   1997
335.43 — dc21   97-119
                                                                                    CIP

Visit our website: www.citylights.com

CITY LIGHTS BOOKS are edited by Lawrence Ferlinghetti and
Nancy J. Peters and published at the City Lights Bookstore,
261 Columbus Avenue, San Francisco, CA 94133.

ACKNOWLEDGMENTS

I am indebted to Sally Soriano, Peggy Noton, Jane Scantlebury, and Richard Plevin for their valuable support and helpful criticisms of the manuscript. On numerous occasions, Jane also utilized her professional librarian skills to track down much needed information at my request. My thanks also to Stephanie Welch, Neala Hazé, and Kathryn Cahill for valuable assistance rendered.

Again, I wish to express my gratitude to Nancy J. Peters, my editor at City Lights Books, for her encouragement and her critical reading of the final text. And belated thanks are owed my publisher, the poet and artist Lawrence Ferlinghetti, for inviting me to become a City Lights author some years ago. Finally, a word of appreciation to Stacey Lewis and others too numerous to mention who partook in the production and distribution of this book: they who do the work.

ACKNOWLEDGEMENTS

To the Reds and others, nameless heroes many,
who resisted yesterday's Blackshirts and who
continue to fight today's ruthless corporate
stuffed shirts.

And to the memory of Sean Gervasi and
Max Gundy, valued friends and warriors for
social justice.

Per chi conosce solo il tuo colore, bandiera rossa,
tu devi realmente esistere, perchè lui esista . . .
tu che già vanti tante glorie borghesi e operaie,
ridiventa straccio, e il più povero ti sventoli.

For him who knows only your color, red flag,
you must really exist, so he may exist . . .
you who already have achieved many bourgeois
                        and working-class glories,
you become a rag again and the poorest wave you.

                                    — *Pier Paolo Pasolini*

CONTENTS

3 LEFT ANTICOMMUNISM 41

Like conservatives and reactionaries, most of the U.S. Left greeted communism in the Soviet Union and Eastern Europe with fear and loathing, and with idealized expectations that took no account of Western encirclement and the survival necessities of socialism under siege.

4 COMMUNISM IN WONDERLAND 59

The internal irrationalities and weaknesses of past communist economies and the systemic reasons why productivity stagnated and reforms were so difficult to effect.

5 STALIN'S FINGERS 76

Newly published documentation on the gulag reveals a somewhat different picture of the repressive nature of communist systems, both in the past and in recent times. The historic accomplishments in economic development within communist countries represented a positive gain in the lives of hundreds of millions.

6 THE FREE-MARKET PARADISE GOES EAST (I) 87

Repression by conservative forces in the former communist states in the name of "democratic reform." Privileges from pre-communist days restored to the old owning classes. Western investors plunder the public sector at great profit to themselves, reducing the former communist countries to Third World levels.

7 THE FREE-MARKET PARADISE GOES EAST (II) 105

The emergence of free-market rapacity and growing inequality, widespread crime, social maladies, and victimization, especially of women, children, the elderly, and the poor. The Third Worldization and cultural decay of formerly collectivist societies.

PREFACE

This book invites those immersed in the prevailing orthodoxy of "democratic capitalism" to entertain iconoclastic views, to question the shibboleths of free-market mythology and the persistence of both right and left anticommunism, and to consider anew, with a receptive but not uncritical mind, the historic efforts of the much maligned Reds and other revolutionaries.

The political orthodoxy that demonizes communism permeates the entire political perspective. Even people on the Left have internalized the liberal/conservative ideology that equates fascism and communism as equally evil totalitaran twins, two major mass movements of the twentieth century. This book attempts to show the enormous differences between fascism and communism both past and present, both in theory and practice, especially in regard to questions of social equality, private capital accumulation, and class interest.

The orthodox mythology also would have us believe that the Western democracies (with the United States leading the way) have opposed both totalitarian systems with equal vigor. In fact, U.S. leaders have been dedicated above all to making the world safe for global corporate investment and the private profit system. Pursuant of this goal, they have used fascism to protect capitalism, while claiming to be saving democracy from communism.

In the pages ahead I discuss how capitalism propagates and profits from fascism, the value of revolution in the advancement of the human condition, the causes and effects of the destruction of communism, the continuing relevance of Marxism and class analysis, and the heartless nature of corporate-class power.

Over a century ago, in his great work *Les Misérables* Victor Hugo asked, "Will the future arrive?" He was thinking of a future of social justice, free from the "terrible shadows" of oppression imposed by the few upon the great mass of humankind. Of late, some scribes have announced "the end of history." With the overthrow of communism, the monumental struggle between alternative systems has ended, they say. Capitalism's victory is total. No great transformations are in the offing. The global free market is here to stay. What you see is what you are going to get, now and always. This time the class struggle is definitely over. So Hugo's question is answered: the future has indeed arrived, though not the one he had hoped for.

This intellectually anemic end-of-history theory was hailed as a brilliant exegesis and accorded a generous reception by commentators and reviewers of the corporate-controlled media. It served the official worldview perfectly well, saying what the higher circles had been telling us for generations: that the struggle between classes is not an everyday reality but an outdated notion, that an untrammeled capitalism is here to stay now and forever, that the future belongs to those who control the present.

But the question we really should be asking is, do we have a future at all? More than ever, with the planet itself at stake, it becomes necessary to impose a reality check on those who would plunder our limited ecological resources in the pursuit of limitless profits, those who would squander away our birthright and extinguish our liberties in their uncompromising pursuit of self-gain.

History teaches us that all ruling elites try to portray themselves as the natural and durable social order, even ones that are in serious crisis, that threaten to devour their environmental base in order to continually recreate their hierarchal structure of power and privilege. And all ruling elites are scornful and intolerant of alternative viewpoints.

Truth is an uncomfortable venue for those who pretend to serve our society while in fact serving only themselves—at our expense. I hope this effort will chip away at the Big Lie. The truth may not set us free, as the Bible claims, but it is an important first step in that direction.

—Michael Parenti

CHAPTER ONE

RATIONAL FASCISM

While walking through New York's Little Italy, I passed a novelty shop that displayed posters and T-shirts of Benito Mussolini giving the fascist salute. When I entered the shop and asked the clerk why such items were being offered, he replied, "Well, some people like them. And, you know, maybe we need someone like Mussolini in this country." His comment was a reminder that fascism survives as something more than a historical curiosity.

Worse than posters or T-shirts are the works by various writers bent on "explaining" Hitler, or "reevaluating" Franco, or in other ways sanitizing fascist history. In Italy, during the 1970s, there emerged a veritable cottage industry of books and articles claiming that Mussolini not only made the trains run on time but also made Italy work well. All these publications, along with many conventional academic studies, have one thing in common: They say little if anything about the class policies of fascist Italy and Nazi Germany. How did these regimes deal with social services, taxes, business, and the conditions of labor? For whose benefit and at whose expense? Most of the literature on fascism and Nazism does not tell us.[1]

Plutocrats Choose Autocrats

Let us begin with a look at fascism's founder. Born in 1883, the son of a blacksmith, Benito Mussolini's early manhood was marked by street brawls, arrests, jailings, and violent radical political activities. Before World War I Mussolini was a socialist. A brilliant organizer, agitator, and gifted journalist, he became editor of the Socialist party's official newspaper. Yet many of his comrades suspected him of being less interested in advancing socialism than in advancing himself. Indeed, when the Italian upper class tempted him with recognition, financial support, and the promise of power, he did not hesitate to switch sides.

By the end of World War I, Mussolini, the socialist, who had organized strikes for workers and peasants had become Mussolini, the fascist, who broke strikes on behalf of financiers and landowners. Using the huge sums he received from wealthy interests, he projected himself onto the national scene as the acknowledged leader of *i fasci di combattimento,* a movement composed of black-shirted ex-army officers and sundry toughs who were guided by no clear political doctrine other than a militaristic patriotism and conservative dislike for anything associated with socialism and organized labor. The fascist Blackshirts spent their time attacking trade unionists, socialists, communists, and farm cooperatives.

---

[1] Among the thousands of titles that deal with fascism, there are a few worthwhile exceptions that do not evade questions of political economy and class power, for instance: Gaetano Salvemini, *Under the Ax of Fascism* (New York: Howard Fertig, 1969); Daniel Guerin, *Fascism and Big Business* (New York: Monad Press/ Pathfinder Press, 1973); James Pool and Suzanne Pool, *Who Financed Hitler* (New York: Dial Press, 1978); Palmiro Togliatti, *Lectures on Fascism* (New York: International Publishers, 1976); Franz Neumann, *Behemoth* (New York: Oxford University Press, 1944); R. Palme Dutt, *Fascism and Social Revolution* (New York: International Publisher, 1935).

After World War I, Italy had settled into a pattern of parliamentary democracy. The low pay scales were improving, and the trains were already running on time. But the capitalist economy was in a postwar recession. Investments stagnated, heavy industry operated far below capacity, and corporate profits and agribusiness exports were declining.

To maintain profit levels, the large landowners and industrialists would have to slash wages and raise prices. The state in turn would have to provide them with massive subsidies and tax exemptions. To finance this corporate welfarism, the populace would have to be taxed more heavily, and social services and welfare expenditures would have to be drastically cut — measures that might sound familiar to us today.

But the government was not completely free to pursue this course. By 1921, many Italian workers and peasants were unionized and had their own political organizations. With demonstrations, strikes, boycotts, factory takeovers, and the forceable occupation of farmlands, they had won the right to organize, along with concessions in wages and work conditions.

To impose a full measure of austerity upon workers and peasants, the ruling economic interests would have to abolish the democratic rights that helped the masses defend their modest living standards. The solution was to smash their unions, political organizations, and civil liberties. Industrialists and big landowners wanted someone at the helm who could break the power of organized workers and farm laborers and impose a stern order on the masses. For this task Benito Mussolini, armed with his gangs of Blackshirts, seemed the likely candidate.[2]

---

[2] Between January and May 1921, "the fascists destroyed 120 labor headquarters, attacked 243 socialist centers and other buildings, killed 202 workers (in addition to 44 killed by the police and gendarmerie), and wounded 1,144." During this time 2,240 workers were arrested and only 162 fascists. In the 1921-22 period up to Mussolini's seizure of state power, "500 labor halls and cooperative stores were burned, and 900 socialist municipalities were dissolved": Dutt, *Fascism and Social Revolution,* 124.

In 1922, the Federazione Industriale, composed of the leaders of industry, along with representatives from the banking and agribusiness associations, met with Mussolini to plan the "March on Rome," contributing 20 million lire to the undertaking. With the additional backing of Italy's top military officers and police chiefs, the fascist "revolution"—really a coup d'état—took place.

Within two years after seizing state power, Mussolini had shut down all opposition newspapers and crushed the Socialist, Liberal, Catholic, Democratic, and Republican parties, which together had commanded some 80 percent of the vote. Labor leaders, peasant leaders, parliamentary delegates, and others critical of the new regime were beaten, exiled, or murdered by fascist terror *squadristi*. The Italian Communist party endured the severest repression of all, yet managed to maintain a courageous underground resistance that eventually evolved into armed struggle against the Blackshirts and the German occupation force.

In Germany, a similar pattern of complicity between fascists and capitalists emerged. German workers and farm laborers had won the right to unionize, the eight-hour day, and unemployment insurance. But to revive profit levels, heavy industry and big finance wanted wage cuts for their workers and massive state subsidies and tax cuts for themselves.

During the 1920s, the Nazi *Sturmabteilung* or SA, the brown-shirted storm troopers, subsidized by business, were used mostly as an antilabor paramilitary force whose function was to terrorize workers and farm laborers. By 1930, most of the tycoons had concluded that the Weimar Republic no longer served their needs and was too accommodating to the working class. They greatly increased their subsidies to Hitler, propelling the Nazi party onto the national stage. Business tycoons supplied the Nazis with generous funds for fleets of motor cars and loudspeakers to saturate the cities and villages of Germany, along with funds for Nazi party organizations, youth groups, and paramilitary forces. In the July

1932 campaign, Hitler had sufficient funds to fly to fifty cities in the last two weeks alone.

In that same campaign the Nazis received 37.3 percent of the vote, the highest they ever won in a democratic national election. They never had a majority of the people on their side. To the extent that they had any kind of reliable base, it generally was among the more affluent members of society. In addition, elements of the petty bourgeoisie and many lumpenproletariats served as strong-arm party thugs, organized into the SA storm troopers. But the great majority of the organized working class supported the Communists or Social Democrats to the very end.

In the December 1932 election, three candidates ran for president: the conservative incumbent Field Marshal von Hindenburg, the Nazi candidate Adolph Hitler, and the Communist party candidate Ernst Thaelmann. In his campaign, Thaelmann argued that a vote for Hindenburg amounted to a vote for Hitler and that Hitler would lead Germany into war. The bourgeois press, including the Social Democrats, denounced this view as "Moscow inspired." Hindenburg was re-elected while the Nazis dropped approximately two million votes in the Reichstag election as compared to their peak of over 13.7 million.

True to form, the Social Democrat leaders refused the Communist party's proposal to form an eleventh-hour coalition against Nazism. As in many other countries past and present, so in Germany, the Social Democrats would sooner ally themselves with the reactionary Right than make common cause with the Reds.[3] Meanwhile a number of right-wing parties coalesced behind the Nazis and in January 1933, just weeks after the election, Hindenburg invited Hitler to become chancellor.

---

[3] Earlier in 1924, Social Democratic officials in the Ministry of Interior used Reichswehr and Free Corps fascist paramilitary troops to attack left-wing demonstrators. They imprisoned seven thousand workers and suppressed Communist party newspapers: Richard Plant, *The Pink Triangle* (New York: Henry Holt, 1986), 47.

Upon assuming state power, Hitler and his Nazis pursued a politico-economic agenda not unlike Mussolini's. They crushed organized labor and eradicated all elections, opposition parties, and independent publications. Hundreds of thousands of opponents were imprisoned, tortured, or murdered. In Germany as in Italy, the communists endured the severest political repression of all groups.

Here were two peoples, the Italians and Germans, with different histories, cultures, and languages, and supposedly different temperaments, who ended up with the same repressive solutions because of the compelling similarities of economic power and class conflict that prevailed in their respective countries. In such diverse countries as Lithuania, Croatia, Rumania, Hungary, and Spain, a similar fascist pattern emerged to do its utmost to save big capital from the impositions of democracy.[4]

Whom Did the Fascists Support?

There is a vast literature on who supported the Nazis, but relatively little on whom the Nazis supported after they came to power. This is in keeping with the tendency of conventional scholarship to avoid the entire subject of capitalism whenever something unfavorable might be said about it. Whose interests did Mussolini and Hitler support?

In both Italy in the 1920s and Germany in the 1930s, old industrial evils, thought to have passed permanently into history, re-emerged as the conditions of labor deteriorated precipitously. In the name of saving society from the Red Menace, unions and strikes were outlawed. Union property and farm cooperatives were confiscated and handed over to rich private owners. Minimum-wage laws, overtime pay, and factory safety regulations were abolished.

---

[4] This is not to gainsay that cultural differences can lead to important variations. Consider, for instance, the horrific role played by anti-Semitism in Nazi Germany as compared to fascist Italy.

Speedups became commonplace. Dismissals or imprisonment awaited those workers who complained about unsafe or inhumane work conditions. Workers toiled longer hours for less pay. The already modest wages were severely cut, in Germany by 25 to 40 percent, in Italy by 50 percent. In Italy, child labor was reintroduced.

To be sure, a few crumbs were thrown to the populace. There were free concerts and sporting events, some meager social programs, a dole for the unemployed financed mostly by contributions from working people, and showy public works projects designed to evoke civic pride.

Both Mussolini and Hitler showed their gratitude to their big business patrons by privatizing many perfectly solvent state-owned steel mills, power plants, banks, and steamship companies. Both regimes dipped heavily into the public treasury to refloat or subsidize heavy industry. Agribusiness farming was expanded and heavily subsidized. Both states guaranteed a return on the capital invested by giant corporations while assuming most of the risks and losses on investments. As is often the case with reactionary regimes, public capital was raided by private capital.

At the same time, taxes were increased for the general populace but lowered or eliminated for the rich and big business. Inheritance taxes on the wealthy were greatly reduced or abolished altogether.

The result of all this? In Italy during the 1930s the economy was gripped by recession, a staggering public debt, and widespread corruption. But industrial profits rose and the armaments factories busily rolled out weapons in preparation for the war to come. In Germany, unemployment was cut in half with the considerable expansion in armaments jobs, but overall poverty increased because of the drastic wage cuts. And from 1935 to 1943 industrial profits increased substantially while the net income of corporate leaders climbed 46 percent. During the radical 1930s, in the United States, Great Britain, and Scandanavia, upper-income groups experienced a modest decline in their share of the national income; but in Germany the top 5 percent enjoyed a 15 percent gain.[5]

Despite this record, most writers have ignored fascism's close collaboration with big business. Some even argue that business was not a beneficiary but a victim of fascism. Angelo Codevilla, a Hoover Institute conservative scribe, blithely announced: "If fascism means anything, it means government ownership and control of business" (*Commentary*, 8/94). Thus fascism is misrepresented as a mutant form of socialism. In fact, if fascism means anything, it means all-out government support for business and severe repression of antibusiness, prolabor forces.[6]

Is fascism merely a dictatorial force in the service of capitalism? That may not be *all* it is, but that certainly is an important part of fascism's raison d'être, the function Hitler himself kept referring to when he talked about saving the industrialists and bankers from Bolshevism. It is a subject that deserves far more attention than it has received.

While the fascists might have believed they were saving the plutocrats from the Reds, in fact the revolutionary Left was never strong enough to take state power in either Italy or Germany. Popular forces, however, were strong enough to cut into profit rates and

---

[5] Simon Kuznets, "Qualitative Aspects of the Economic Growth of Nations," *Economic Development and Cultural Change*, 5, no. 1, 1956, 5-94.

[6] Ex-leftist and reborn conservative Eugene Genovese (*New Republic*, 4/1/95) eagerly leaped to the conclusion that it is a "nonsensical interpretation" to see "fascism as a creature of big capital." Genovese was applauding Eric Hobsbawm, who argued that the capitalist class was not the primary force behind fascism in Spain. In response, Vicente Navarro (*Monthly Review* 1/96 and 4/96) noted that the "major economic interests of Spain," assisted by at least one Texas oil millionaire and other elements of international capital, did indeed finance Franco's fascist invasion and coup against the Spanish Republic. A crucial source, Navarro writes, was the financial empire of Joan March, founder of the Liberal Party and owner of a liberal newspaper. Considered a modernizer and an alternative to the oligarchic, land-based, reactionary sector of capital, March made common cause with these same oligarchs once he saw that working-class parties were gaining strength and his own economic interests were being affected by the reformist Republic.

interfere with the capital accumulation process. This frustrated capitalism's attempts to resolve its internal contradictions by shifting more and more of its costs onto the backs of the working populace. Revolution or no revolution, this democratic working-class resistance was troublesome to the moneyed interests.

Along with serving the capitalists, fascist leaders served themselves, getting in on the money at every opportunity. Their personal greed and their class loyalties were two sides of the same coin. Mussolini and his cohorts lived lavishly, cavorting within the higher circles of wealth and aristocracy. Nazi officials and SS commanders amassed personal fortunes by plundering conquered territories and stealing from concentration camp inmates and other political victims. Huge amounts were made from secretly owned, well-connected businesses, and from contracting out camp slave labor to industrial firms like I.G. Farben and Krupp.

Hitler is usually portrayed as an ideological fanatic, uninterested in crass material things. In fact, he accumulated an immense fortune, much of it in questionable ways. He expropriated art works from the public domain. He stole enormous sums from Nazi party coffers. He invented a new concept, the "personality right," that enabled him to charge a small fee for every postage stamp with his picture on it, a venture that made him hundreds of millions of marks.[7]

The greatest source of Hitler's wealth was a secret slush fund to which leading German industrialists regularly donated. Hitler "knew that as long as German industry was making money, his private money sources would be inexhaustible. Thus, he'd see to it that German industry was never better off than under his rule—by launching, for one thing, gigantic armament projects,"[8] or what we today would call fat defense contracts.

---

[7] There already was a stamp of von Hindenburg to honor his presidency. Old Hindenburg, who had no love for Hitler, sarcastically said he would make Hitler his postal minister, because "then he can lick my backside."

[8] Wulf Schwarzwaeller, *The Unknown Hitler* (Bethesda, Md.: National Press Books, 1989), 197.

Far from being the ascetic, Hitler lived self-indulgently. During his entire tenure in office he got special rulings from the German tax office that allowed him to avoid paying income or property taxes. He had a motor pool of limousines, private apartments, country homes, a vast staff of servants, and a majestic estate in the Alps. His happiest times were spent entertaining European royalty, including the Duke and Duchess of Windsor, who numbered among his enthusiastic admirers.

Kudos for Adolph and Benito

Italian fascism and German Nazism had their admirers within the U.S. business community and the corporate-owned press. Bankers, publishers, and industrialists, including the likes of Henry Ford, traveled to Rome and Berlin to pay homage, receive medals, and strike profitable deals. Many did their utmost to advance the Nazi war effort, sharing military-industrial secrets and engaging in secret transactions with the Nazi government, even after the United States entered the war.[9] During the 1920s and early 1930s, major publications like *Fortune,* the *Wall Street Journal, Saturday Evening Post, New York Times, Chicago Tribune,* and *Christian Science Monitor* hailed Mussolini as the man who rescued Italy from anarchy and radicalism. They spun rhapsodic fantasies of a resurrected Italy where poverty and exploitation had suddenly disappeared, where Reds had been vanquished, harmony reigned, and Blackshirts protected a "new democracy."

The Italian-language press in the United States eagerly joined the chorus. The two most influential newspapers, *L'Italia* of San Francisco, financed largely by A.P. Giannini's Bank of America, and *Il Progresso* of New York, owned by multimillionaire Generoso Pope, looked favorably on the fascist regime and suggested that the United States could benefit from a similar social order.

---

[9] Charles Higham, *Trading with the Enemy* (New York: Dell, 1983).

Some dissenters refused to join the "We Adore Benito" chorus. The *Nation* reminded its readers that Mussolini was not *saving* democracy but *destroying* it. Progressives of all stripes and various labor leaders denounced fascism. But their critical sentiments received little exposure in the U.S. corporate media.

As with Mussolini, so with Hitler. The press did not look too unkindly upon *der Fuehrer's* Nazi dictatorship. There was a strong "Give Adolph A Chance" contingent, some of it greased by Nazi money. In exchange for more positive coverage in the Hearst newspapers, for instance, the Nazis paid almost ten times the standard subscription rate for Hearst's INS wire service. In return, William Randolph Hearst instructed his correspondents in Germany to file friendly reports about Hitler's regime. Those who refused were transferred or fired. Hearst newspapers even opened their pages to occasional guest columns by prominent Nazi leaders like Alfred Rosenberg and Hermann Göring.

By the mid to late 1930s, Italy and Germany, allied with Japan, another industrial latecomer, were aggressively seeking a share of the world's markets and colonial booty, an expansionism that brought them increasingly into conflict with more established Western capitalist nations like Great Britain, France, and the United States. As the clouds of war gathered, U.S. press opinion about the Axis powers took on a decisively critical tone.

The Rational Use of Irrational Ideology

Some writers stress the "irrational" features of fascism. By doing so, they overlook the rational politico-economic functions that fascism performed. Much of politics is the rational manipulation of irrational symbols. Certainly, this is true of fascist ideology, whose emotive appeals have served a class-control function.

First there was the cult of the leader, in Italy: *il Duce,* in Germany: *der Feuhrerprinzip.* With leader-worship there came the idolatry of the state. As Mussolini wrote, "The Fascist conception of life stresses the importance of the State and accepts the individual only insofar as his interests coincide with those of the State." Fascism preaches the authoritarian rule of an all-encompassing state and a supreme leader. It extols the harsher human impulses of conquest and domination, while rejecting egalitarianism, democracy, collectivism, and pacifism as doctrines of weakness and decadence.

A dedication to peace, Mussolini wrote, "is hostile to fascism." Perpetual peace, he claimed in 1934, is a "depressing" doctrine. Only in "cruel struggle" and "conquest" do men or nations achieve their highest realization. "Though words are beautiful things," he asserted, "rifles, machine guns, planes, and cannons are still more beautiful." And on another occasion he wrote: "War alone . . . puts the stamp of nobility upon the peoples who have the courage to meet it." Ironically, most Italian army conscripts had no stomach for Mussolini's wars, tending to remove themselves from battle once they discovered that the other side was using live ammunition.

Fascist doctrine stresses monistic values: *Ein Volk, ein Reich, ein Fuehrer* (one people, one rule, one leader). The people are no longer to be concerned with class divisions but must see themselves as part of a harmonious whole, rich and poor as one, a view that supports the economic status quo by cloaking the ongoing system of class exploitation. This is in contrast to a left agenda that advocates the articulation of popular demands and a sharpened awareness of social injustice and class struggle.

This monism is buttressed by atavistic appeals to the mythical roots of the people. For Mussolini, it was the grandeur that was Rome; for Hitler, the ancient Volk. A play written by a pro-Nazi, Hans Jorst, entitled *Schlageter* and performed widely throughout Germany soon after the Nazis seized power (Hitler attended the opening night in Berlin) pits Volk mysticism against class politics. The enthusiastic August is talking to his father, Schneider:

August: You won't believe it, Papa but . . . the young people don't pay much attention to these old slogans anymore . . . the class struggle is dying out.

Schneider: So, and what do you have then?

August: The Volk community.

Schneider: And that's a slogan?

August: No, it's an experience!

Schneider: My God, our class struggle, our strikes, they weren't an experience, eh? Socialism, the International, were they fantasies maybe?

August: They were necessary, but . . . they are historical experiences.

Schneider: So, and the future therefore will have your Volk community. Tell me how do you actually envision it? Poor, rich, healthy, upper, lower, all this ceases with you, eh? . . .

August: Look, Papa, upper, lower, poor, rich, that always exists. It is only the importance one places on that question that's decisive. To us life is not chopped up into working hours and furnished with price charts. Rather, we believe in human existence as a whole. None of us regards making money as the most important thing; we want to serve. The individual is a corpuscle in the bloodstream of his people.[10]

The son's comments are revealing: "the class struggle is dying out." Papa's concern about the abuses of class power and class injustice is facilely dismissed as just a frame of mind with no objective reality. It is even falsely equated with a crass concern for money. ("None of us regard making money as important.") Presumably matters of wealth are to be left to those who have it. We have something better, August is saying: a totalistic, monistic experience as a people, all of us, rich and poor, working together for some greater glory. Conveniently overlooked is how the "glorious sacrifices" are borne by the poor for the benefit of the rich.

The position enunciated in that play and in other Nazi propaganda does not reveal an indifference to class; quite the contrary, it represents a keen awareness of class interests, a well-engineered

---

[10] George Mosse (ed.), *Nazi Culture* (New York: Grosset & Dunlap, 1966), 116-118.

effort to mask and mute the strong class consciousness that existed among workers in Germany. In the crafty denial, we often find the hidden admission.

Patriarchy and Pseudo-Revolution

Fascism's national chauvinism, racism, sexism, and patriarchal values also served a conservative class interest. Fascist doctrine, especially the Nazi variety, makes an explicit commitment to racial supremacy. Human attributes, including class status, are said to be inherited through blood; one's position in the social structure is taken as a measure of one's innate nature. Genetics and biology are marshalled to justify the existing class structure, not unlike what academic racists today are doing with their "bell curve" theories and warmed-over eugenics claptrap.

Along with race and class inequality, fascism supports homophobia and sexual inequality. Among Nazism's earliest victims were a group of Nazi homosexuals, leaders of the SA storm troopers. When complaints about the openly homosexual behavior of SA leader Ernst Roehm and some of his brown-shirted storm troopers continued to reach Hitler after he seized power, he issued an official statement contending that the issue belonged "purely to the private domain" and that an SA officer's "private life cannot be an object of scrutiny unless it conflicts with basic principles of National Socialist ideology."

The paramilitary SA had been used to win the battle of the streets against trade unionists and Reds. The storm troopers acted as a pseudo-revolutionary force that appealed to mass grievances with a rhetorical condemnation of finance capital. When SA membership skyrocketed to three million in 1933, this was too discomforting to the industrial barons and military patricians. SA street brawlers who denounced bourgeois decadence and called for sharing the wealth and completing the "Nazi revolution" would have to be dealt with.

Having used the SA to take state power, Hitler then used the state

to neutralize the SA. Now suddenly Roehm's homosexuality did conflict with National Socialist ideology. In truth, the SA had to be
decapitated not because its leaders were homosexual—though that
was the reason given—but because it threatened to turn into a serious problem. Roehm and about 300 other SA members were executed, not all of whom were gay. Among the victims was veteran Nazi
propagandist Gregor Strasser, who was suspected of leftist leanings.

Of course, many Nazis were virulently homophobic. One of the
most powerful of all, SS leader Heinrich Himmler, saw homosexuals
as a threat to German manhood and the moral fiber of Teutonic peoples, for a "homosexual sissy" would not procreate or make a good
soldier. Himmler's homophobia and sexism came together when he
announced: "If a man just looks at a girl in America, he can be forced
to marry her or pay damages . . . therefore men protect themselves in
the USA by turning to homosexuals. Women in the USA are like bat-
tle-axes—they hack away at males."[11] Thus spoke one of the great
minds of Nazism. In time, Himmler succeeded in extending the
oppression of gays beyond the SA leadership. Thousands of gay civilians perished in SS concentration camps.

In societies throughout the ages, if able to find the opportunity,
women have attempted to limit the number of children they bear.
This poses a potential problem for a fascist patriarchy that needs vast
numbers of soldiers and armaments workers. Women are less able to
assert their procreative rights if kept subservient and dependent. So
fascist ideology extolled patriarchal authority. Every man must be a
husband, a father, and a soldier, il Duce said. Woman's greatest calling was to cultivate her domestic virtues, devotedly tending to the
needs of her family while bearing as many offspring for the state as
she could.

Patriarchal ideology was linked to a conservative class ideology
that saw all forms of social equality as a threat to hierarchal control

---

[11] Richard Plant, *The Pink Triangle*, 91.

and privilege. The patriarchy buttressed the plutocracy: If women get out of line, what will happen to the family? And if the family goes, the entire social structure is threatened. What then will happen to the state and to the dominant class's authority, privileges, and wealth? The fascists were big on what today is called "family values"—though most of the top Nazi leaders could hardly be described as devoted family men.

In Nazi Germany, racism and anti-Semitism served to misdirect legitimate grievances toward convenient scapegoats. Anti-Semitic propaganda was cleverly tailored to appeal to different audiences. Superpatriots were told that the Jew was an alien internationalist. Unemployed workers were told that their nemesis was the Jewish capitalist and Jewish banker. For debtor farmers, it was the Jewish usurer. For the middle class, it was the Jewish union leader and Jewish communist. Here again we have a consciously rational use of irrational images. The Nazis might have been crazy but they were not stupid.

What distinguishes fascism from ordinary right-wing patriarchal autocracies is the way it attempts to cultivate a revolutionary aura. Fascism offers a beguiling mix of revolutionary-sounding mass appeals and reactionary class politics. The Nazi party's full name was the National Socialist German Workers Party, a left-sounding name. As already noted, the SA storm troopers had a militant share-the-wealth strain in their ranks that was suppressed by Hitler after he took state power.

Both the Italian fascists and the Nazis made a conscious effort to steal the Left's thunder. There were mass mobilizations, youth organizations, work brigades, rallies, parades, banners, symbols, and slogans. There was much talk about a "Nazi revolution" that would revitalize society, sweeping away the old order and building the new.

For this reason, mainstream writers feel free to treat fascism and communism as totalitarian twins. It is a case of reducing essence to form. The similarity in form is taken as reason enough to blur the vast difference in actual class content. Writers like A. James Gregor and William Ebenstein, countless Western political leaders, and others who supposedly are on the democratic Left, regularly lump fascism with communism. Thus, Noam Chomsky claims, "The rise of corporations was in fact a manifestation of the same phenomena that led to fascism and Bolshevism, which sprang out of the same totalitarian soil."[12] But in the Italy and Germany of that day, most workers and peasants made a firm distinction between fascism and communism, as did industrialists and bankers who supported fascism out of fear and hatred of communism, a judgment based largely on class realities.

Years ago, I used to say that fascism never succeeded in solving the irrational contradictions of capitalism. Today I am of the opinion that it did accomplish that goal—but only for the capitalists, not for the populace. Fascism never intended to offer a social solution that would serve the general populace, only a reactionary one, forcing all the burdens and losses onto the working public. Divested of its ideological and organizational paraphernalia, fascism is nothing more than a final solution to the class struggle, the totalistic submergence and exploitation of democratic forces for the benefit and profit of higher financial circles.

Fascism is a false revolution. It cultivates the appearance of popular politics and a revolutionary aura without offering a genuine revolutionary class content. It propagates a "New Order" while serving the same old moneyed interests. Its leaders are not guilty of confusion but of deception. That they work hard to mislead the public does not mean they themselves are misled.

Friendly to Fascism

One of the things conveniently overlooked by mainstream writers is the way Western capitalist states have cooperated with fascism. In his collaborationist efforts, British Prime Minister Neville

---

[12] Chomsky interviewed by Husayn Al-Kurdi, *Perception*, March/April 1996.

Chamberlain was positively cozy with the Nazis. He and many of his class saw Hitler as a bulwark against communism in Germany, and Nazi Germany as a bulwark against communism in Europe.

After World War II, the Western capitalist allies did little to eradicate fascism from Italy or Germany, except for putting some of the top leaders on trial at Nuremberg. By 1947, German conservatives began to depict the Nuremberg prosecutors as dupes of the Jews and communists. In Italy, the strong partisan movement that had waged armed struggle against fascism was soon treated as suspect and unpatriotic. Within a year after the war, almost all Italian fascists were released from prison while hundreds of communists and other leftist partisans who had been fighting the Nazi occupation were jailed. History was turned on its head, transforming the Blackshirts into victims and the Reds into criminals. Allied authorities assisted in these measures.[13]

Under the protection of U.S. occupation authorities, the police, courts, military, security agencies, and bureaucracy remained largely staffed by those who had served the former fascist regimes or by their ideological recruits—as is true to this day. The perpetrators of the Holocaust murdered six million Jews, half a million Gypsies, thousands of homosexuals, several million Ukranians, Russians, Poles, and others, and got away with it—in good part because the very people who were supposed to investigate these crimes were themselves complicit.

---

[13] Roy Palmer Domenico, *Italian Fascists on Trial, 1943-1948* (Chapel Hill: University of North Carolina Press, 1991), passim. So in France, very few of the Vichy collaborators were purged. "No one of any rank was seriously punished for his or her role in the roundup and deportation of Jews to Nazi camps": Herbert Lottman, *The Purge* (New York: William Morrow, 1986), 290. Much the same can be said about Germany; see Ingo Muller, *Hitler's Justice* (Cambridge, Mass.: Harvard University Press, 1991), part 3, "The Aftermath." U.S. military authorities restored fascist collaborators to power in various Far East nations. In South Korea, for instance, Koreans collaborators and the Japanese-trained police were used to suppress left democratic forces. The South Korean Army was commanded by officers who had served in the Imperial Japanese Army "and were proud of it." Numbers of them had been guilty of war crimes in the Philippines and China: Hugh Deane, "Korea, China and the United States: A Look Back," *Monthly Review,* Feb. 1995, 20 and 23.

In comparison, when the Communists took over in East Germany, they removed some 80 percent of the judges, teachers, and officials for their Nazi collaboration; they imprisoned thousands, and they executed six hundred Nazi party leaders for war crimes. They would have shot more of the war criminals had not so many fled to the protective embrace of the West.

What happened to the U.S. businesses that collaborated with fascism? The Rockefeller family's Chase National Bank used its Paris office in Vichy France to help launder German money to facilitate Nazi international trade during the war, and did so with complete impunity.[14] Corporations like DuPont, Ford, General Motors, and ITT owned factories in enemy countries that produced fuel, tanks, and planes that wreaked havoc on Allied forces. After the war, instead of being prosecuted for treason, ITT collected $27 million from the U.S. government for war damages inflicted on its German plants by Allied bombings. General Motors collected over $33 million. Pilots were given instructions not to hit factories in Germany that were owned by U.S. firms. Thus Cologne was almost leveled by Allied bombing but its Ford plant, providing military equipment for the Nazi army, was untouched; indeed, German civilians began using the plant as an air raid shelter.[15]

For decades, U.S. leaders have done their part in keeping Italian fascism alive. From 1945 to 1975, U.S. government agencies gave an estimated $75 million to right-wing organizations in Italy, including some with close ties to the neofascist *Movimento Sociale Italiano* (MSI). In 1975, then Secretary of State Henry Kissinger met with

---

[14] After the war, Hermann Abs, head of the Deutsche Bank and in effect "Hitler's paymaster," was hailed by David Rockefeller as "the most important banker of our time." According to his *New York Times* obituary, Abs "played a dominant role in West Germany's reconstruction after World War II." Neither the *Times* nor Rockefeller said a word about Abs' Nazi connections, his bank's predatory incursions across Nazi occupied Europe, and his participation, as a board member of I.G. Farben, in the use of slave labor at Auschwitz: Robert Carl Miller, *Portland Free Press*, Sept/Oct 1994.

[15] Charles Higham, *Trading with the Enemy*.

MSI leader Giorgio Almirante in Washington to discuss what "alternatives" might be considered should the Italian Communists win the elections and take control of the government.

Hundreds of Nazi war criminals found a haven in the United States, either living in comfortable anonymity or actively employed by U.S. intelligence agencies during the cold war and otherwise enjoying the protection of high-placed individuals. Some of them found their way onto the Republican presidential campaign committees of Richard Nixon, Ronald Reagan, and George Bush.[16]

In Italy, from 1969 to 1974, high-ranking elements in Italian military intelligence and civilian intelligence agencies; members of P2, a secret lodge of upper-class reactionaries, pro-fascist Vatican officials, and top military brass; and GLADIO, a NATO-inspired anticommunist mercenary force, embarked upon a concerted campaign of terror and sabotage known as the "strategy of tension." Other participants included a secret neofascist group called the Ordine Nuovo, NATO officials, members of the carabinieri, mafia bosses, thirty generals, eight admirals, and influential Freemasons like Licio Gelli (a fascist war criminal recruited by U.S. intelligence in 1944). The terrorism was aided and abetted by the "international security apparatus," including the CIA. In 1995, the CIA refused to cooperate with an Italian parliamentary commission investigating the strategy of tension (*Corriere della Sera*, 4/12/95, 5/29/95).

The terrorist conspirators carried out a series of kidnappings,

---

[16] One of them, Boleslavs Maikovskis, a Latvian police chief who fled to West Germany to escape Soviet war crimes investigations and then to the United States, was heavily implicated in the Nazi slaughter of over two hundred Latvian villagers. He served for a time on a Republican party subcommittee to re-elect President Nixon, then fled back to Germany to avoid a belated U.S. war crimes investigation, dying at the ripe old age of 92 (*New York Times*, 5/8/96). Nazi war criminals have been aided by Western intelligence agencies, business interests, the military, and even the Vatican. In October 1944, German paratroop commander Major Walter Reder slaughtered 1,836 defenseless civilians in a village near Bologna, Italy as a reprisal against Partisan activities. He was released from prison in 1985, after Pope John Paul II, among others, made an appeal on his behalf—over the strenuous protests of relatives of the victims.

assassinations, and bombing massacres (*i stragi*), including the explosion that killed eighty-five people and injured some two hundred, many seriously, in the Bologna train station in August 1980. As subsequent judicial investigations concluded, the strategy of tension was not a simple product of neofascism but the consequence of a larger campaign conducted by state security forces against the growing popularity of the democratic parliamentary Left. The objective was to "combat by any means necessary the electoral gains of the Italian Communist party" and create enough fear and terror in the population so as to undermine the multiparty social democracy and replace it with an authoritarian "presidential republic," or in any case "a stronger and more stable executive." (*La Repubblica*, 4/9/95; *Corriere della Sera*, 3/27/95, 3/28/95, 5/29/95).

In the 1980s, scores of people were murdered in Germany, Belgium and elsewhere in Western Europe by extreme rightists in the service of state security agencies (*Z Magazine*, March 1990). These acts of terrorism went mostly unreported in the U.S. corporate-owned media. As with the earlier strategy of tension in Italy, the attacks were designed to create enough popular fear and uncertainty so as to undermine the existing social democracies.

Authorities in these Western European countries and the United States have done little to expose neo-Nazi networks. As the whiffs of fascism develop into an undeniable stench, we are reminded that Hitler's progeny are still with us and that they have dangerous links with each other and within the security agencies of various Western capitalist nations.

In Italy, in 1994, the national elections were won by the National Alliance, a broadened version of the neofascist MSI, in coalition with a league of Northern separatists, and Forza Italia, a quasi-fascist movement headed by industrialist and media tycoon Silvio Berlusconi. The National Alliance played on resentments regarding unemployment, taxes, and immigration. It called for a single tax rate for rich and poor alike, school vouchers, a stripping away of the social benefits, and the privatization of most services.

The Italian neofascists were learning from the U.S. reactionaries how to achieve fascism's class goals within the confines of quasi-democratic forms: use an upbeat, Reaganesque optimism; replace the jackbooted militarists with media-hyped crowd pleasers; convince people that government is the enemy—especially its social service sector—while strengthening the repressive capacities of the state; instigate racist hostility and antagonisms between the resident population and immigrants; preach the mythical virtues of the free market; and pursue tax and spending measures that redistribute income upward.

Conservatives in the Western nations utilize diluted forms of the fascist mass appeal. In the USA, they propagate populist-sounding appeals to the "ordinary Middle American" while quietly pressing for measures that serve the interests of the wealthiest individuals and corporations. In 1996, right-wing Speaker of the House of Representatives Newt Gingrich, while proffering a new rollback agenda that supposedly would revitalize all of society, announced "I am a genuine revolutionary." Whether in Italy, Germany, the United States, or any other country, when the Right offers a "new revolution" or a "new order," it is in the service of the same old moneyed interests, leading down that well-trodden road of reaction and repression that so many Third World countries have been forced to take, the road those at the top want us all to travel.

CHAPTER 2

LET US NOW PRAISE REVOLUTION

For most of this century U.S. foreign policy has been devoted to the suppression of revolutionary governments and radical movements around the world. The turn of the twentieth century found the McKinley administration in a war of attrition against the people of the Philippines lasting from 1898 to 1902 (with pockets of resistance continuing for years afterward). In that conflict, U.S. forces slaughtered some 200,000 Filipino women, men, and children.[1] At about that same time, in conjunction with various European colonial powers, the United States invaded China to help suppress the Boxer Rebellion at substantial loss of life to the Chinese rebels. U.S. forces took over Hawaii, Cuba, Puerto Rico, and Guam and in the following decades invaded Mexico, Soviet Russia, Nicaragua, Honduras, the Dominican Republic, and other countries, actions that usually inflicted serious losses upon the populations of these countries.

---

[1] Leon Wolf, *Little Brown Brother* (New York: Oxford University Press, 1960).

The Costs of Counterrevolution

From grade school through grad school, few of us are taught anything about these events, except to be told that U.S. forces must intervene in this or that country in order to protect U.S. interests, thwart aggression, and defend our national security. U.S. leaders fashioned other convenient rationales for their interventions abroad. The public was told that the peoples of various countries were in need of our civilizing guidance and desired the blessings of democracy, peace, and prosperity. To accomplish this, of course, it might be necessary to kill off considerable numbers of the more recalcitrant among them. Such were the measures our policymakers were willing to pursue in order to "uplift lesser peoples."

The emergence of major communist powers like the Soviet Union and the Peoples Republic of China lent another dimension to U.S. global counterrevolutionary policy. The communists were depicted as evil incarnate, demonized conspirators who sought power for power's sake. The United States had to be everywhere to counteract this spreading "cancer," we were told.

In the name of democracy, U.S. leaders waged a merciless war against revolutionaries in Indochina for the better part of twenty years. They dropped many times more tons of explosives on Vietnam than were used throughout World War II by all combatants combined. Testifying before a Congressional committee, former CIA director William Colby admitted that under his direction U.S. forces and their South Vietnam collaborators carried out the selective assassination of 24,000 Vietnamese dissidents, in what was known as the Phoenix Program. His associate, the South Vietnamese minister of information, maintained that 40,000 was a more accurate estimate.[2] U.S. policymakers and their media mouthpieces judged the war a "mistake" because the Vietnamese proved incapable of being properly instructed by B-52 bomber raids and death squads. By

---

[2] Mark Lane, *Plausible Denial* (New York: Thunder's Mouth Press, 1991), 79.

prevailing against this onslaught, the Vietnamese supposedly demonstrated that they were "unprepared for our democratic institutions."

In pursuit of counterrevolution and in the name of freedom, U.S. forces or U.S.-supported surrogate forces slaughtered 2,000,000 North Koreans in a three-year war; 3,000,000 Vietnamese; over 500,000 in aerial wars over Laos and Cambodia; over 1,500,000 in Angola; over 1,000,000 in Mozambique; over 500,000 in Afghanistan; 500,000 to 1,000,000 in Indonesia; 200,000 in East Timor; 100,000 in Nicaragua (combining the Somoza and Reagan eras); over 100,000 in Guatemala (plus an additional 40,000 disappeared); over 700,000 in Iraq;[3] over 60,000 in El Salvador; 30,000 in the "dirty war" of Argentina (though the government admits to only 9,000); 35,000 in Taiwan, when the Kuomintang military arrived from China; 20,000 in Chile; and many thousands in Haiti, Panama, Grenada, Brazil, South Africa, Western Sahara, Zaire, Turkey, and dozens of other countries, in what amounts to a free-market world holocaust.

Official sources either deny these U.S.-sponsored mass murders or justify them as necessary measures that had to be taken against an implacable communist foe. Anticommunist propaganda saturated our airwaves, schools, and political discourse. Despite repeated and often factitious references to the tyranny of the Red Menace, the anticommunist opinion makers never spelled out what communists actually did in the way of socio-economic policy. This might explain why, despite decades of Red-bashing propaganda, most Americans, including many who number themselves among the political cognoscenti, still cannot offer an informed statement about the social policies of communist societies.

---

[3] The 1991 war waged by the Bush administration against Iraq, which claimed an estimated 200,000 victims, was followed by U.S.-led United Nations economic sanctions. A study by the United Nations Food and Agriculture Organization, *The Children Are Dying* (1996), reports that since the end of the war 576,000 Iraqi children have died of starvation and disease and tens of thousands more suffer defects and illnesses due to the five years of sanctions.

The anti-Red propagandists uttered nary a word about how revolutionaries in Russia, China, Cuba, Vietnam, Nicaragua, and other countries nationalized the lands held by rich exploitative landlords and initiated mass programs for education, health, housing, and jobs. Not a word about how their efforts advanced the living standards and life chances of hundreds of millions in countries that had long suffered under the yoke of feudal oppression and Western colonial pillage, an improvement in mass well-being never before witnessed in history.

No matter that the revolutionaries in various Asian, African, and Latin American countries enjoyed popular support and were willing to pursue a neutralist course in East-West relations rather than place themselves under the hegemony of either Moscow or Peking. They still were targeted for a counterrevolutionary battering. From opposing communists because they might be revolutionaries, it was a short step to opposing revolutionaries because they might be communists.

The real sin of revolutionaries, communist or not, was that they championed the laboring classes against the wealthy few. They advocated changes in the distribution of class power and the way wealth was produced and used. They wanted less individualistic advancement at the expense of the many and collective betterment for the entire working populace.

Presumptions of Power

Ruling classes throughout the world hate and fear communism not for its lack of political democracy, but because it attempts to establish economic democracy by building an egalitarian, collectivist social system—though they rarely come right out and say as much. This counterrevolutionary interventionist policy rests on several dubious assumptions that might be stated and rebutted as follows:

1. "U.S. leaders have the right to define the limits of socioeconomic development within other nations." Not true. Under no

canon of international law or any other legal stricture do the leaders of this country have the right to ordain what kind of economic system or mode of social development another country may adopt, no more right than do the leaders of other countries have to dictate such things to the United States. In practice, the option to dictate is exercised by the strong over the weak, a policy of might, not right.

2. "The United States must play a counterrevolutionary containment role in order to protect our national interests." This is true only if we equate "our national interests" with the investment interests of high finance. U.S. interventionism has been very effective in building neo-imperialism, keeping the land, labor, natural resources, and markets of Third World countries available at bargain prices to multinational corporations. But these corporate interests do not represent the interests of the U.S. people. The public pays for the huge military budgets and endures the export of its jobs to foreign labor markets, the inflow of thousands of impoverished immigrants who compete for scarce employment and housing, and various other costs of empire.[4]

Furthermore, revolutionary governments like Cuba, Libya, Vietnam, and North Korea were—and still are—eager to trade and maintain peaceful relations with this country. These countries do not threaten the national security of the United States or its people, but the overseas interests of global capitalism. If allowed to multiply in numbers, countries with an alternative socialist system, one that uses the land, labor, capital, and natural resources in collectivist ways, placing people before profits, would eventually undermine global capitalism.

3. "The United States has a moral obligation to guarantee the stability of nations that are undergoing democratic development but are threatened by revolutionaries and terrorists." In fact, most U.S. interventions are on behalf of corrupt and self-serving oligarchs and

---

[4] For a further discussion of this and related points, see my book *Against Empire* (San Francisco: City Lights Books, 1995), chapter 4.

antidemocratic militarists (who take power with or without the benefit of U.S.-sponsored showcase elections). Third World oligarchs are frequently educated at elite U.S. universities or end up on the CIA payroll, as do their police chiefs and military officers, many of whom receive training in torture and assassination at U.S. counterinsurgency institutions.[5]

4. "Fundamental social change should be peacefully pursued within the established order of nations rather than by revolutionary turmoil." U.S. policymakers maintain that they favor eliminating mass poverty in poorer countries and that they are not opposed to the laudatory objectives of social revolution but to its violent methods. They say that transformations must be effected gradually and peacefully, preferably through private investment and the benign workings of the free market. In fact, corporate investment is more likely to deter rather than encourage reform by preempting markets and restructuring the local economy to fit foreign capital extraction needs. International finance capital has no interest in bettering the life chances of Third World peoples. Generally, as Western investments have increased in the Third World, life conditions for the ordinary peasants and workers have grown steadily more desperate.

Whose Violence?

People throughout the world do not need more corporate investments, rather they need the opportunity to wrest back their land, labor, natural resources, and markets in order to serve their own social needs. Such a revolutionary development invites fierce opposition from apostles of the free market, whose violent resistance to social change makes peaceful transformation impossible to contemplate.

Even in countries like the United States, where reforms of limited scope have been achieved without revolution, the "peaceful" means

---

[5] On the U.S. training of torturers and assassins, see *Washington Post,* 9/21/96.

employed have entailed popular struggle and turmoil—and a considerable amount of violence and bloodshed, almost all of it inflicted by police and security forces.

That last point frequently goes unmentioned in discussions about the ethics of revolutionary violence. The very concept of "revolutionary violence" is somewhat falsely cast, since most of the violence comes from those who attempt to prevent reform, not from those struggling for reform. By focusing on the violent rebellions of the downtrodden, we overlook the much greater repressive force and violence utilized by the ruling oligarchs to maintain the status quo, including armed attacks against peaceful demonstrations, mass arrests, torture, destruction of opposition organizations, suppression of dissident publications, death squad assassinations, the extermination of whole villages, and the like.

Most social revolutions begin peaceably. Why would it be otherwise? Who would not prefer to assemble and demonstrate rather than engage in mortal combat against pitiless forces that enjoy every advantage in mobility and firepower? Revolutions in Russia, China, Vietnam, and El Salvador all began peacefully, with crowds of peasants and workers launching nonviolent protests only to be met with violent oppression from the authorities. Peaceful protest and reform are exactly what the people are denied by the ruling oligarchs. The dissidents who continue to fight back, who try to defend themselves from the oligarchs' repressive fury, are then called "violent revolutionaries" and "terrorists."

For those local and international elites who maintain control over most of the world's wealth, social revolution is an abomination. Whether it be peaceful or violent is a question of no great moment to them. Peaceful reforms that infringe upon their profitable accumulations and threaten their class privileges are as unacceptable to them as the social upheaval imposed by revolution.

Reforms that advance the conditions of life for the general public are not as materially intractable or as dependent on capital resources as we have been led to believe. There is no great mystery to building a health clinic, or carrying out programs for food rationing, land redistribution, literacy, jobs, and housing. Such tasks are well within the capacity of any state—if there is the political will and a mobilization of popular class power.

Consider Kerala, a state in India where the actions of popular organizations and mass movements have won important victories over the last forty years against politico-economic oppression, generating a level of social development considerably better than that found in most of the Third World, and accomplished without outside investment. Kerala has mass literacy, a lower birth rate and lower death rate than the rest of India, better public health services, fewer child workers, higher nutritional levels (thanks to a publicly subsidized food rationing system), more enlightened legal support and educational programs for women, and some social security protections for working people and for the destitute and physically handicapped. In addition, the people of Kerala radically altered a complex and exploitative system of agrarian relations and won important victories against the more horrid forms of caste oppression.

Though Kerala has no special sources of wealth, it has had decades of communist organizing and political struggle that reached and moved large numbers of people and breathed life into the state's democracy. "Despite its relatively short periods in the leadership of government . . . it is the Communist party that has set the basic legislative agenda of the people of Kerala," notes Indian scholar V.K. Ramachandran (*Monthly Review*, 5/95). All this is not to deny that many people in Kerala endure unacceptable conditions of poverty. Still, despite a low level of income and limited resources, the achievements wrought by democratic government intervention—and propelled by mass action—have been substantial, representing the difference between a modestly supportable existence and utter misery.

Many Third World peoples produce dedicated and capable popular organizations, as did the communists in Kerala, but they are usually destroyed by repressive state forces. In Kerala, popular agitation and input took advantage of democratic openings and in turn gave more social substance to the democracy. What is needed for social betterment is not International Monetary Fund loans or corporate investments but political organization and democratic opportunity, and freedom from U.S.-sponsored state terrorism.

U.S. foreign aid programs offer another example of how imperialist policy masquerades as social reform within Third World nations. Aid programs are not intended to effect serious social betterment. At best, they finance piecemeal projects of limited impact. More often, they are used to undermine local markets, drive small farmers off their land, build transportation and office facilities needed by outside investors, increase a country's debt and economic dependency, and further open its economy to multinational corporate penetration.

Free Market for the Few

Third World revolutionaries are branded as the enemies of stability. "Stability" is a code word for a society in which privileged social relations are securely entrenched. When popular forces mobilize against privilege and wealth, this causes "instability," which is judged to be undesirable by U.S. policymakers and their faithful flacks in the U.S. corporate media.

Here we have a deceptive state of affairs. What poses as a U.S. commitment to peaceful nonviolent change is really a commitment to the violent defense of an unjust, undemocratic, global capitalism. The U.S. national security state uses coercion and violence not in support of social reform but against it, all in the name of "stability," "counterterrorism," "democracy,"—and of late and more honestly, "the free market."

When he was head of the State Department policy planning staff during the early years of the cold war, the noted author George

Kennan revealed the ruthless realpolitik mentality of those dedicated to social inequality within and between nations. Kennan maintained that a wealthy United States facing an impoverished world could not afford "the luxury of altruism and world benefaction" and should cease talking about "vague and unreal objectives such as human rights, the raising of the living standards, and democratization. . . . The less we are hampered by idealistic slogans, the better" (PPS23, U.S. State Department, Feburary 1948). Speaking at a briefing for U.S. ambassadors to Latin America, Kennan remarked: "The final answer might be an unpleasant one, but we should not hesitate before police repression by the local government. This is not shameful since the Communists are essentially traitors. . . . It is better to have a strong [i.e., repressive] regime in power than a liberal government if it is indulgent and relaxed and penetrated by Communists." In a 1949 State Department intelligence report, Kennan wrote that communists were "people who are committed to the belief that the government has direct responsibility for the welfare of the people." So they had to be dealt with harshly without regard for such niceties as democratization and human rights.

It is said that the United States cannot renege on its commitments to other peoples and must continue as world leader; the rest of the world expects that of us. But the ordinary peoples of the world have never called for U.S. world leadership. Quite the contrary, they usually want the United States to go home and leave them to their own affairs. This is because U.S. commitments are not to the ordinary people of other lands, but to the privileged reactionary factions that are most accomodating to Western investors. As Kennan's remarks indicate, the U.S. policymaking establishment has been concerned not with advancing the welfare of impoverished peoples around the world but with defeating whoever allies themselves with the common people, be they Reds or not.

Whatever their grave shortcomings, do not U.S.-supported Third World rulers represent something better than the kind of tyranny that communists and revolutionary totalitarians bring? Academic cheerleaders for U.S. interventionism, such as Samuel P. Huntington of Harvard University, think so: "However bad a given evil may be, a worse one is always possible and often likely," Huntington concludes, going on to defend as "lesser evils" the murderous regimes in Chile under Pinochet and South Africa under apartheid.[6]

We might recall Jean Kirkpatrick's distinction between "benign" authoritarian right-wing governments that supposedly are not all that brutal and allow gradual change, and horrid totalitarian left-wing ones that suppress everyone. The real distinction is that the right-wing government maintains the existing privileged order of the free market, keeping the world safe for the empowered hierarchies and wealthy classes of the world. In contrast, the left-wing "totalitarians" want to abolish exploitative property relations and create a more egalitarian economic system. Their favoring the have-nots over the haves is what makes them so despicable in the eyes of the latter.

U.S. leaders claim to be offended by certain features of social revolutionary governments, such as one-party rule and the coercive implementation of revolutionary change. But one-party autocracy is acceptable if the government is rightist, that is, friendly toward private corporate investment as in Turkey, Zaire, Guatemala, Indonesia, and dozens of other countries (including even communist countries that are sliding down the free-market path, such as China).

We might recall that unforgettable moment when President George

---

[6] *American Political Science Review,* 82, March 1988, 5. In that same statement, Huntington describes Mangosutho Buthelezi, the CIA-supported head of the South African Inkatha Freedom Party, as a "notable contemporary democratic reformer." It is a matter of public record that Buthelezi collaborated with the top-level apartheid military and police in the murder of thousands of African National Congress (ANC) supporters. Colonel Eugene de Kock, the highest ranking officer convicted of apartheid crimes, who once described himself as the government's most efficient assassin, testified that he had supplied weapons, vehicles, and training to Buthelezi's organization for a "total onslaught" strategy against democratic, anti-apartheid forces (AP report, *San Francisco Chronicle,* 9/18/96). There is no denying that Buthelezi is Huntington's kind of guy.

Bush—whose invasions of Panama and Iraq brought death and destruction to those nations and who presided over a U.S. military empire that is the single greatest purveyor of violence in the world—lectured revolutionary leader Nelson Mandela on the virtues of nonviolence, even going so far as to quote Martin Luther King, Jr., during Mandela's visit to Washington, D.C. in June 1990. Mandela's real sin in Bush's eyes was that he was part of a revolutionary movement that engaged in armed struggle against a violently repressive apartheid regime in South Africa. Bush's capacity for selective perception had all the unexamined audacity of a dominant ideology that condemns only those who act *against* an unjust status quo, not those who use violence to preserve it. It would have come as a great relief to people around the world if the president of the United States had adopted a policy of nonviolence for his own government. In fact, he had done no such thing.

The Freedom of Revolution

U.S. politico-economic leaders may find revolutionary reforms undesirable, but most people who live in revolutionary societies find them preferable to the old regimes and worth defending. The Bay of Pigs invasion of Cuba was a fiasco not because of "insufficient air coverage" but because the Cuban people closed ranks behind their government and threw back the invaders.

Another "captive people," the North Vietnamese, acted in similar fashion in the early 1970s. Instead of treating the severe destruction and disruptions caused by the U.S. aerial war against their country as a golden opportunity to overthrow "Hanoi's yoke," they continued to support their beleaguered government at great sacrifice to themselves. And in South Vietnam, the National Liberation Front enjoyed tactical opportunities for supply and surprise, largely because it was supported by people in the countryside and cities.

During the Vietnam era, explanations as to why people sided with the communist revolutionaries came from some unexpected sources. U.S. ambassador Henry Cabot Lodge admitted, "The only people who have been doing anything for the little man—to lift him up—have been the communists" (*New York Times*, 2/27/66). In a similar vein, one faithful propagator of the official line, columnist James Reston, wrote with surprising candor, "Even Premier Ky [U.S.-sponsored dictator of South Vietnam] told this reporter today that the communists were closer to the people's yearnings for social justice and an independent life than his own government" (*New York Times*, 9/1/65). What Lodge and Reston left unsaid was that the "little man" and the "people's yearnings" for social justice were the very things that U.S. leaders were bent on suppressing.

Some people conclude that anyone who utters a good word about leftist one-party revolutions must harbor antidemocratic or "Stalinist" sentiments. But to applaud social revolutions is not to oppose political freedom. To the extent that revolutionary governments construct substantive alternatives for their people, they increase human options and freedom.

There is no such thing as freedom in the abstract. There is freedom to speak openly and iconoclastically, freedom to organize a political opposition, freedom of opportunity to get an education and pursue a livelihood, freedom to worship as one chooses or not worship at all, freedom to live in healthful conditions, freedom to enjoy various social benefits, and so on. Most of what is called freedom gets its definition within a social context.

Revolutionary governments extend a number of popular freedoms without destroying those freedoms that never existed in the previous regimes. They foster conditions necessary for national self-determination, economic betterment, the preservation of health and human life, and the end of many of the worst forms of ethnic, patriarchal, and class oppression. Regarding patriarchal oppression, consider the vastly improved condition of women in revolutionary Afghanistan and South Yemen before the counterrevolutionary repression in the 1990s, or in Cuba after the 1959 revolution as compared to before.

U.S. policymakers argue that social revolutionary victory anywhere represents a diminution of freedom in the world. The assertion is false. The Chinese Revolution did not crush democracy; there was none to crush in that oppressively feudal regime. The Cuban Revolution did not destroy freedom; it destroyed a hateful U.S.-sponsored police state. The Algerian Revolution did not abolish national liberties; precious few existed under French colonialism. The Vietnamese revolutionaries did not abrogate individual rights; no such rights were available under the U.S.-supported puppet governments of Bao Dai, Diem, and Ky.

Of course, revolutions do limit the freedoms of the corporate propertied class and other privileged interests: the freedom to invest privately without regard to human and environmental costs, the freedom to live in obscene opulence while paying workers starvation wages, the freedom to treat the state as a private agency in the service of a privileged coterie, the freedom to employ child labor and child prostitutes, the freedom to treat women as chattel, and so on.

Today, no one in U.S. policy circles worries about the politico-economic oppression suffered in dozens of right-wing client states. Their professed desire to bring Western political democracy to nations that have had revolutions rarely extends to free-market autocracies. And the grudging moves toward political democracy occasionally made in these autocracies come only through popular pressure and rebellion and only with the unspoken understanding that democratic governance will not infringe substantially upon the interests of the moneyed class.

What Measure of Pain?

Is the pain of revolution worth the gain? Cost-benefit accounting is a complicated business when applied to social transitions. But have we ever bothered to compare the violence of revolution against the violence that preceded it? "I do not know how one measures the price of historical victories," said Robert Heilbroner, "I only know that the way in which we ordinarily keep the books of history is wrong." We make no tally of the generations claimed by that combination of economic exploitation and political suppression so characteristic of the ancien regimes: the hapless victims of flood and famine in the Yangtze valley of yesterday, the child prostitutes found dead in the back alleys of old Shanghai, the muzhiks stricken by cold and starvation across the frozen steppes of Russia.

And what of today? No one is tallying the thousands of nameless victims who succumb to U.S.-trained torturers in Latin America, the hundreds of villages burned by counterinsurgency forces, the millions who are driven from their ancestral lands and sentenced to permanently stunted and malnourished lives, the millions more who perish in the desperate misery and congestion of shanty slums and internment camps. Their sufferings go unrecorded and are not figured in the balance when the revolution metes out justice to erstwhile oligarchs and oppressors or commits excesses and abuses of its own.

And how do we measure the pain of the tens of millions of children throughout the world, many as young as six and seven, who are forced to work seventy hours a week confined in ill-lit, poorly ventilated workshops, under conditions reminiscent of the most horrific days of the Industrial Revolution? The General Agreement on Tariffs and Trade (GATT), a sweeping multinational free-trade act that amounts to a carte blanche for global capitalism, offers no protection for children who are exploited, abused, overworked, and underpaid. During GATT negotiations, leaders of Third World countries successfully argued against placing any restrictions on child labor, arguing that children have always worked in their cultures and such traditional practices should be respected. To prohibit child labor would limit the free market and effect severe hardship on those poor families in which a child is often the only wage earner.

Even if the longstanding practice of children helping out on farms is acceptable (assuming they are not overworked and are allowed to go to school), the practice of "locking them into a hotbox of a factory for 14 hours a day" is something else. Furthermore, they may be the only wage earner "because adult workers have been laid off in favor of children, who are infinitely more exploitable and provide bigger profits for prosperous factory owners" (Anna Quindlen, *New York Times*, 11/23/94).

Traveling across Cuba in 1959, immediately after the overthrow of the U.S.-supported right-wing Batista dictatorship, Mike Faulkner witnessed "a spectacle of almost unrelieved poverty." The rural population lived in makeshift shacks without minimal sanitation. Malnourished children went barefoot in the dirt and suffered "the familiar plague of parasites common to the Third World." There were almost no doctors or schools. And through much of the year, families that depended solely on the seasonal sugar harvest lived close to starvation (*Monthly Review*, 3/96). How does that victimization in prerevolutionary Cuba measure against the much more widely publicized repression that came after the revolution, when Castro's communists executed a few hundred of the previous regime's police assassins and torturers, drove assorted upper-class moneybags into exile, and intimidated various other opponents of radical reforms into silence?

Today, Cuba is a different place. For all its mistakes and abuses, the Cuban Revolution brought sanitation, schools, health clinics, jobs, housing, and human services to a level not found throughout most of the Third World and in many parts of the First World. Infant mortality in Cuba has dropped from 60 per 1000 in 1960 to 9.7 per 1000 by 1991, while life expectancy rose from 55 to 75 in that same period. Smallpox, malaria, tuberculosis, typhoid, polio, and numerous other diseases have been wiped out by improved living standards and public health programs.[7] Cuba has enjoyed a level of literacy higher than in the United States and a life expectancy that compares well with advanced industrial nations (*NACLA Report on the Americas*, September/October 1995). Other peoples besides the Cubans have benefited. As Fidel Castro tells it:

> The [Cuban] revolution has sent teachers, doctors, and workers to dozens of Third World countries without charging a penny. It shed its own blood fighting colonialism, fighting apartheid, and fascism. . . . At one point we had 25,000 Third World students studying on scholarships. We still have many scholarship students from Africa and other countries. In addition, our country has treated more children [13,000] who were victims of the Chernobyl tragedy than all other countries put together.
>
> They don't talk about that, and that's why they blockade us—the country with the most teachers per capita of all countries in the world, including developed countries. The country with the most doctors per capita of all countries [one for every 214 inhabitants]. The country with the most art instructors per capita of all countries in the world. The country with the most sports instructors in the world. That gives you an idea of the effort involved. A country where life expectancy is more than 75 years.
>
> Why are they blockading Cuba? Because no other country has done more for its people. It's the hatred of the ideas that Cuba represents. (*Monthly Review*, 6/95).

Cuba's sin in the eyes of global capitalists is not its "lack of democracy." Most Third World capitalist regimes are far more repressive. Cuba's real sin is that it has tried to develop an alternative to the global capitalist system, an egalitarian socio-economic order that placed corporate property under public ownership, abolished capitalist investors as a class entity, and put people before profits and national independence before IMF servitude.

So a conservative think tank like the Heritage Foundation rated Cuba along with Laos, Iraq, and North Korea as countries with the

---

[7] Theodore MacDonald, *Hippocrates in Havana: Cuba's Health Care System* (1995).

lowest level of "economic freedom." Countries with a high level of economic freedom were those that imposed little or no taxes or regulations on business, and did without wage protections, price controls, environmental safeguards, and benefits for the poor. Economic freedom is the real concern of conservatives and plutocrats; the freedom to utilize vast sums of money to accumulate still vaster sums, regardless of the human and environmental costs.

Mass productivity coupled with elitist distribution results in more wealth for the few and greater poverty for the many. So after two centuries of incredible technological development and unprecedented economic expansion, the number of people living in poverty in the capitalist world has grown more quickly than any other demographic cohort. The world's slum population has increased at a far greater rate than the total global population. Amazing growth in industrial productivity has been accompanied by increasingly desperate want, misery, and repression. In short, there is a causal link between vast concentrations of wealth and widespread poverty. The next time someone preaches the free-market gospel of economic freedom and productivity, we need ask, for whose benefit and at whose cost?

Those who show concern for the elites overthrown in the whirl of revolution should also keep in mind the hundreds of millions more who are obliterated by economic reactionism. If all rebellions were to be successfully repressed today and forever, free-market autocracy's violence against humanity would be with us more unrestrained than ever—as is indeed happening. For these reasons, those of us who are genuinely concerned about democracy, social justice, and the survival of our planet should support rather than oppose popular revolutions.

CHAPTER 3

LEFT ANTICOMMUNISM

In the United States, for over a hundred years, the ruling interests tirelessly propagated anticommunism among the populace, until it became more like a religious orthodoxy than a political analysis. During the cold war, the anticommunist ideological framework could transform any data about existing communist societies into hostile evidence. If the Soviets refused to negotiate a point, they were intransigent and belligerent; if they appeared willing to make concessions, this was but a skillful ploy to put us off our guard. By opposing arms limitations, they would have demonstrated their aggressive intent; but when in fact they supported most armament treaties, it was because they were mendacious and manipulative. If the churches in the USSR were empty, this demonstrated that religion was suppressed; but if the churches were full, this meant the people were rejecting the regime's atheistic ideology. If the workers went on strike (as happened on infrequent occasions), this was evidence of their alienation from the collectivist system; if they didn't go on strike, this was because they were intimidated and lacked freedom. A scarcity of consumer goods demonstrated the failure of the economic system; an improvement in consumer supplies meant only that the leaders were attempting to placate a restive population and so maintain a firmer hold over them.

If communists in the United States played an important role struggling for the rights of workers, the poor, African-Americans, women, and others, this was only their guileful way of gathering support among disfranchised groups and gaining power for themselves. How one gained power by fighting for the rights of powerless groups was never explained. What we are dealing with is a nonfalsifiable orthodoxy, so assiduously marketed by the ruling interests that it affected people across the entire political spectrum.

Genuflection to Orthodoxy

Many on the U.S. Left have exhibited a Soviet bashing and Red baiting that matches anything on the Right in its enmity and crudity. Listen to Noam Chomsky holding forth about "left intellectuals" who try to "rise to power on the backs of mass popular movements" and "then beat the people into submission. . . . You start off as basically a Leninist who is going to be part of the Red bureaucracy. You see later that power doesn't lie that way, and you very quickly become an ideologist of the right. . . . We're seeing it right now in the [former] Soviet Union. The same guys who were communist thugs two years back, are now running banks and [are] enthusiastic free marketeers and praising Americans" (*Z Magazine,* 10/95).

Chomsky's imagery is heavily indebted to the same U.S. corporate political culture he so frequently criticizes on other issues. In his mind, the revolution was betrayed by a coterie of "communist thugs" who merely hunger for power rather than wanting the power to end hunger. In fact, the communists did not "very quickly" switch to the Right but struggled in the face of a momentous onslaught to keep Soviet socialism alive for more than seventy years. To be sure, in the Soviet Union's waning days some, like Boris Yeltsin, crossed over to capitalist ranks, but others continued to resist free-market incursions at great cost to themselves, many meeting their deaths during Yeltsin's violent repression of the Russian parliament in 1993.

Some leftists and others fall back on the old stereotype of power-hungry Reds who pursue power for power's sake without regard for actual social goals. If true, one wonders why, in country after country, these Reds side with the poor and powerless often at great risk and sacrifice to themselves, rather than reaping the rewards that come with serving the well-placed.

For decades, many left-leaning writers and speakers in the United States have felt obliged to establish their credibility by indulging in anticommunist and anti-Soviet genuflection, seemingly unable to give a talk or write an article or book review on whatever political subject without injecting some anti-Red sideswipe. The intent was, and still is, to distance themselves from the Marxist-Leninist Left.

Adam Hochschild, a liberal writer and publisher, warned those on the Left who might be lackadaisical about condemning existing communist societies that they "weaken their credibility" (*Guardian*, 5/23/84). In other words, to be credible opponents of the cold war, we first had to join in cold war condemnations of communist societies. Ronald Radosh urged that the peace movement purge itself of communists so that it not be accused of being communist (*Guardian*, 3/16/83). If I understand Radosh: To save ourselves from anticommunist witchhunts, we should ourselves become witchhunters.

Purging the Left of communists became a longstanding practice, having injurious effects on various progressive causes. For instance, in 1949 some twelve unions were ousted from the CIO because they had Reds in their leadership. The purge reduced CIO membership by some 1.7 million and seriously weakened its recruitment drives and political clout. In the late 1940s, to avoid being "smeared" as Reds, Americans for Democratic Action (ADA), a supposedly progressive group, became one of the most vocally anticommunist organizations.

The strategy did not work. ADA and others on the Left were still attacked for being communist or soft on communism by those on the Right. Then and now, many on the Left have failed to realize that those who fight for social change on behalf of the less-privileged elements of society will be Red-baited by conservative elites whether they are communists or not. For ruling interests, it makes little difference whether their wealth and power is challenged by "communist subversives" or "loyal American liberals." All are lumped together as more or less equally abhorrent.

Even when attacking the Right, left critics cannot pass up an opportunity to flash their anticommunist credentials. So Mark Green writes in a criticism of President Ronald Reagan that "when presented with a situation that challenges his conservative catechism, like an unyielding Marxist-Leninist, [Reagan] will change not his mind but the facts."[1] While professing a dedication to fighting dogmatism "both of the Right and Left," individuals who perform such de rigueur genuflections reinforce the anticommunist dogma. Red-baiting leftists contributed their share to the climate of hostility that has given U.S. leaders such a free hand in waging hot and cold wars against communist countries and which even today makes a progressive or even liberal agenda difficult to promote.

A prototypic Red-basher who pretended to be on the Left was George Orwell. In the middle of World War II, as the Soviet Union was fighting for its life against the Nazi invaders at Stalingrad, Orwell announced that a "willingness to criticize Russia and Stalin is *the* test of intellectual honesty. It is the only thing that from a literary intellectual's point of view is really dangerous" (*Monthly Review*, 5/83). Safely ensconced within a virulently anticommunist society, Orwell (with Orwellian doublethink) characterized the condemnation of communism as a lonely courageous act of defiance. Today, his ideological progeny are still at it, offering themselves as intrepid left critics of the Left, waging a valiant struggle against imaginary Marxist-Leninist-Stalinist hordes.

---

[1] Mark Green and Gail MacColl, New York: Pantheon Books, *There He Goes Again: Ronald Reagan's Reign of Error* (1983), 12.

Sorely lacking within the U.S. Left is any rational evaluation of the Soviet Union, a nation that endured a protracted civil war and a multinational foreign invasion in the very first years of its existence, and that two decades later threw back and destroyed the Nazi beast at enormous cost to itself. In the three decades after the Bolshevik revolution, the Soviets made industrial advances equal to what capitalism took a century to accomplish—while feeding and schooling their children rather than working them fourteen hours a day as capitalist industrialists did and still do in many parts of the world. And the Soviet Union, along with Bulgaria, the German Democratic Republic, and Cuba, provided vital assistance to national liberation movements in countries around the world, including Nelson Mandela's African National Congress in South Africa.

Left anticommunists remained studiously unimpressed by the dramatic gains won by masses of previously impoverished people under communism. Some were even scornful of such accomplishments. I recall how in Burlington Vermont, in 1971, the noted anticommunist anarchist, Murray Bookchin, derisively referred to my concern for "the poor little children who got fed under communism" (his words).

Slinging Labels

Those of us who refused to join in the Soviet bashing were branded by left anticommunists as "Soviet apologists" and "Stalinists," even if we disliked Stalin and his autocratic system of rule and believed there were things seriously wrong with existing Soviet society.[2] Our real sin was that unlike many on the Left we

---

[2] In the first edition of my book *Inventing Reality* (New York: St. Martin's Press, 1986) I wrote: "The U.S. media's encompassing negativity in regard to the Soviet Union might induce some of us to react with an unqualifiedly glowing view of that society. The truth is, in the USSR there exist serious problems of labor productivity, industrialization, urbanization, bureaucracy, corruption, and alcoholism. There are production and distribution bottlenecks, plan failures, consumer scarcities, criminal abuses of power, suppression of dissidents, and expressions of alienation among some persons in the population."

refused to uncritically swallow U.S. media propaganda about communist societies. Instead, we maintained that, aside from the well-publicized deficiencies and injustices, there were positive features about existing communist systems that were worth preserving, that improved the lives of hundreds of millions of people in meaningful and humanizing ways. This claim had a decidedly unsettling effect on left anticommunists who themselves could not utter a positive word about any communist society (except possibly Cuba) and could not lend a tolerant or even courteous ear to anyone who did.[3]

Saturated by anticommunist orthodoxy, most U.S. leftists have practiced a left McCarthyism against people who did have something positive to say about existing communism, excluding them from participation in conferences, advisory boards, political endorsements, and left publications. Like conservatives, left anticommunists tolerated nothing less than a blanket condemnation of the Soviet Union as a Stalinist monstrosity and a Leninist moral aberration.[4]

That many U.S. leftists have scant familiarity with Lenin's writings and political work does not prevent them from slinging the "Leninist" label. Noam Chomsky, who is an inexhaustible fount of anticommunist caricatures, offers this comment about Leninism: "Western and also Third World intellectuals were attracted to the

---

[3] Many on the U.S. Left, who displayed only hostility and loathing toward the Soviet Union and other European communist states, have a warm feeling for Cuba, which they see as having a true revolutionary tradition and a somewhat more open society. In fact, at least until the present (January 1997), Cuba has had much the same system as the USSR and other communist nations: public ownership of industry, a planned economy, close relations with existing communist nations, and one-party rule—with the party playing a hegemonic role in the government, media, labor unions, women's federations, youth groups, and other institutions.

[4] Partly in reaction to the ubiquitous anticommunist propaganda that permeated U.S. media and public life, many U.S. communists, and others close to them, refrained from criticizing the autocratic features of the Soviet Union. Consequently, they were accused of thinking that the USSR was a worker's "paradise" by critics who seemingly would settle for nothing less than paradisial standards. After the Khrushchev revelations in 1953, U.S. communists grudgingly allowed that Stalin had made "mistakes" and even had committed crimes.

Bolshevik counterrevolution [*sic*] because Leninism is, after all, a doctrine that says that the radical intelligentsia have a right to take state power and to run their countries by force, and that is an idea which is rather appealing to intellectuals."[5] Here Chomsky fashions an image of power-hungry intellectuals to go along with his cartoon image of power-hungry Leninists, villains seeking not the revolutionary means to fight injustice but power for power's sake. When it comes to Red-bashing, some of the best and brightest on the Left sound not much better than the worst on the Right.

At the time of the 1996 terror bombing in Oklahoma City, I heard a radio commentator announce: "Lenin said that the purpose of terror is to terrorize." U.S. media commentators have repeatedly quoted Lenin in that misleading manner. In fact, his statement was *disapproving* of terrorism. He polemicized against isolated terrorist acts which do nothing but create terror among the populace, invite repression, and isolate the revolutionary movement from the masses. Far from being the totalitarian, tight-circled conspirator, Lenin urged the building of broad coalitions and mass organizations, encompassing people who were at different levels of political development. He advocated whatever diverse means were needed to advance the class struggle, including participation in parliamentary elections and existing trade unions. To be sure, the working class, like any mass group, needed organization and leadership to wage a successful revolutionary struggle, which was the role of a vanguard party, but that did not mean the proletarian revolution could be fought and won by putschists or terrorists.

Lenin constantly dealt with the problem of avoiding the two extremes of liberal bourgeois opportunism and ultra-left adventurism. Yet he himself is repeatedly identified as an ultra-left putschist by mainstream journalists and some on the Left. Whether Lenin's approach to revolution is desirable or even relevant today is a question

---

[5] Chomsky interviewed by Husayn Al-Kurdi: *Perception,* March/April 1996.

that warrants critical examination. But a useful evaluation is not likely to come from people who misrepresent his theory and practice.[6]

Left anticommunists find any association with communist organizations morally unacceptable because of the "crimes of communism." Yet many of them are themselves associated with the Democratic party in this country, either as voters or as members, apparently unconcerned about the morally unacceptable political crimes committed by leaders of that organization. Under one or another Democratic administration, 120,000 Japanese Americans were torn from their homes and livelihoods and thrown into detention camps; atomic bombs were dropped on Hiroshima and Nagasaki with an enormous loss of innocent life; the FBI was given authority to infiltrate political groups; the Smith Act was used to imprison leaders of the Trotskyist Socialist Workers Party and later on leaders of the Communist party for their political beliefs; detention camps were established to round up political dissidents in the event of a "national emergency"; during the late 1940s and 1950s, eight thousand federal workers were purged from government because of their political associations and views, with thousands more in all walks of life witchhunted out of their careers; the Neutrality Act was used to impose an embargo on the Spanish Republic that worked in favor of Franco's fascist legions; homicidal counterinsurgency programs were initiated in various Third World countries; and the Vietnam War was pursued and escalated. And for the better part of a century, the Congressional leadership of the Democratic party protected racial segregation and stymied all anti-lynching and fair employment bills. Yet all these crimes, bringing ruination and death to many, have not moved the liberals, the social democrats, and the "democratic socialist" anticommunists to insist

---

[6] I refer the reader to Lenin's books: *The State and Revolution; "Left-Wing" Communism—an Infantile Disorder; What is to Be Done?*, and various articles and statements still available in collected editions. See also John Ehrenberg's treatment of Marxism-Leninism in his *The Dictatorship of the Proletariat, Marxism's Theory of Socialist Democracy* (New York: Routledge, 1992).

repeatedly that we issue blanket condemnations of either the
Democratic party or the political system that produced it, certainly
not with the intolerant fervor that has been directed against existing
communism.

Pure Socialism vs. Siege Socialism

The upheavals in Eastern Europe did not constitute a defeat for
socialism because socialism never existed in those countries, according to some U.S. leftists. They say that the communist states offered
nothing more than bureaucratic, one-party "state capitalism" or
some such thing. Whether we call the former communist countries
"socialist" is a matter of definition. Suffice it to say, they constituted
something different from what existed in the profit-driven capitalist
world—as the capitalists themselves were not slow to recognize.

First, in communist countries *there was less economic inequality
than under capitalism.* The perks enjoyed by party and government
elites were modest by corporate CEO standards in the West, as were
their personal incomes and life styles. Soviet leaders like Yuri
Andropov and Leonid Brezhnev lived not in lavishly appointed man-
sions like the White House, but in relatively large apartments in a
housing project near the Kremlin set aside for government leaders.
They had limousines at their disposal (like most other heads of state)
and access to large dachas where they entertained visiting dignitaries.
But they had none of the immense personal wealth that most U.S.
leaders possess.

The "lavish life" enjoyed by East Germany's party leaders, as
widely publicized in the U.S. press, included a $725 yearly allowance
in hard currency, and housing in an exclusive settlement on the out-
skirts of Berlin that sported a sauna, an indoor pool, and a fitness
center shared by all the residents. They also could shop in stores that
carried Western goods such as bananas, jeans, and Japanese electronics. The U.S. press never pointed out that ordinary East Germans

had access to public pools and gyms and could buy jeans and electronics (though usually not of the imported variety). Nor was the "lavish" consumption enjoyed by East German leaders contrasted to the truly opulent life style enjoyed by the Western plutocracy.

Second, in communist countries, *productive forces were not organized for capital gain and private enrichment; public ownership of the means of production supplanted private ownership.* Individuals could not hire other people and accumulate great personal wealth from their labor. Again, compared to Western standards, differences in earnings and savings among the populace were generally modest. The income spread between highest and lowest earners in the Soviet Union was about five to one. In the United States, the spread in yearly income between the top multibillionaires and the working poor is more like 10,000 to 1.

Third, *priority was placed on human services.* Though life under communism left a lot to be desired and the services themselves were rarely the best, communist countries did guarantee their citizens some minimal standard of economic survival and security, including guaranteed education, employment, housing, and medical assistance.

Fourth, *communist countries did not pursue the capital penetration of other countries.* Lacking a profit motive as their motor force and therefore having no need to constantly find new investment opportunities, they did not expropriate the lands, labor, markets, and natural resources of weaker nations, that is, they did not practice economic imperialism. The Soviet Union conducted trade and aid relations on terms that generally were favorable to the Eastern European nations and Mongolia, Cuba, and India.

All of the above were organizing principles for every communist system to one degree or another. None of the above apply to free-market countries like Honduras, Guatemala, Thailand, South Korea, Chile, Indonesia, Zaire, Germany, or the United States.

But a real socialism, it is argued, would be controlled by the workers themselves through direct participation instead of being run by

Leninists, Stalinists, Castroites, or other ill-willed, power-hungry, bureaucratic cabals of evil men who betray revolutions. Unfortunately, this "pure socialism" view is ahistorical and nonfalsifiable; it cannot be tested against the actualities of history. It compares an ideal against an imperfect reality, and the reality comes off a poor second. It imagines what socialism would be like in a world far better than this one, where no strong state structure or security force is required, where none of the value produced by workers needs to be expropriated to rebuild society and defend it from invasion and internal sabotage.

The pure socialists' ideological anticipations remain untainted by existing practice. They do not explain how the manifold functions of a revolutionary society would be organized, how external attack and internal sabotage would be thwarted, how bureaucracy would be avoided, scarce resources allocated, policy differences settled, priorities set, and production and distribution conducted. Instead, they offer vague statements about how the workers themselves will directly own and control the means of production and will arrive at their own solutions through creative struggle. No surprise then that the pure socialists support every revolution except the ones that succeed.

The pure socialists had a vision of a new society that would create and be created by new people, a society so transformed in its fundaments as to leave little opportunity for wrongful acts, corruption, and criminal abuses of state power. There would be no bureaucracy or self-interested coteries, no ruthless conflicts or hurtful decisions. When the reality proves different and more difficult, some on the Left proceed to condemn the real thing and announce that they "feel betrayed" by this or that revolution.

The pure socialists see socialism as an ideal that was tarnished by communist venality, duplicity, and power cravings. The pure socialists oppose the Soviet model but offer little evidence to demonstrate that other paths could have been taken, that other models of socialism—not created from one's imagination but developed through actual historical experience—could have taken hold and worked better. Was an open, pluralistic, democratic socialism actually possible at this historic juncture? The historical evidence would suggest it was not. As the political philosopher Carl Shames argued:

> How do [the left critics] know that the fundamental problem was the "nature" of the ruling [revolutionary] parties rather than, say, the global concentration of capital that is destroying all independent economies and putting an end to national sovereignty everywhere? And to the extent that it was, where did this "nature" come from? Was this "nature" disembodied, disconnected from the fabric of the society itself, from the social relations impacting on it? . . . Thousands of examples could be found in which the centralization of power was a necessary choice in securing and protecting socialist relations. In my observation [of existing communist societies], the positive of "socialism" and the negative of "bureaucracy, authoritarianism and tyranny" interpenetrated in virtually every sphere of life. (Carl Shames, correspondence to me, 1/15/92.)

The pure socialists regularly blame the Left itself for every defeat it suffers. Their second-guessing is endless. So we hear that revolutionary struggles fail because their leaders wait too long or act too soon, are too timid or too impulsive, too stubborn or too easily swayed. We hear that revolutionary leaders are compromising or adventuristic, bureaucratic or opportunistic, rigidly organized or insufficiently organized, undemocratic or failing to provide strong leadership. But always the leaders fail because they do not put their trust in the "direct actions" of the workers, who apparently would withstand and overcome every adversity if only given the kind of leadership available from the left critic's own groupuscule. Unfortunately, the critics seem unable to apply their own leadership genius to producing a successful revolutionary movement in their own country.

Tony Febbo questioned this blame-the-leadership syndrome of the pure socialists:

It occurs to me that when people as smart, different, dedicated and heroic as Lenin, Mao, Fidel Castro, Daniel Ortega, Ho Chi Minh and Robert Mugabe—and the millions of heroic people who followed and fought with them—all end up more or less in the same place, then something bigger is at work than who made what decision at what meeting. Or even what size houses they went home to after the meeting. . . .

These leaders weren't in a vacuum. They were in a whirlwind. And the suction, the force, the power that was twirling them around has spun and left this globe mangled for more than 900 years. And to blame this or that theory or this or that leader is a simple-minded substitute for the kind of analysis that Marxists [should make]. (*Guardian,* 11/13/91)

To be sure, the pure socialists are not entirely without specific agendas for building the revolution. After the Sandinistas overthrew the Somoza dictatorship in Nicaragua, an ultra-left group in that country called for direct worker ownership of the factories. The armed workers would take control of production without benefit of managers, state planners, bureaucrats, or a formal military. While undeniably appealing, this worker syndicalism denies the necessities of state power. Under such an arrangement, the Nicaraguan revolution would not have lasted two months against the U.S.-sponsored counterrevolution that savaged the country. It would have been unable to mobilize enough resources to field an army, take security measures, or build and coordinate economic programs and human services on a national scale.

Decentralization vs. Survival

For a people's revolution to survive, it must seize state power and use it to (a) break the stranglehold exercised by the owning class over the society's institutions and resources, and (b) withstand the reactionary counterattack that is sure to come. The internal and external dangers a revolution faces necessitate a centralized state power that is not particularly to anyone's liking, not in Soviet Russia in 1917, nor in Sandinista Nicaragua in 1980.

Engels offers an apposite account of an uprising in Spain in 1872-73 in which anarchists seized power in municipalities across the country. At first, the situation looked promising. The king had abdicated and the bourgeois government could muster but a few thousand ill-trained troops. Yet this ragtag force prevailed because it faced a thoroughly parochialized rebellion. "Each town proclaimed itself as a sovereign canton and set up a revolutionary committee (junta)," Engels writes. "[E]ach town acted on its own, declaring that the important thing was not cooperation with other towns but separation from them, thus precluding any possibility of a combined attack [against bourgeois forces]." It was "the fragmentation and isolation of the revolutionary forces which enabled the government troops to smash one revolt after the other."[7]

Decentralized parochial autonomy is the graveyard of insurgency — which may be one reason why there has never been a successful anarcho-syndicalist revolution. Ideally, it would be a fine thing to have only local, self-directed, worker participation, with minimal bureaucracy, police, and military. This probably would be the development of socialism, were socialism ever allowed to develop unhindered by counterrevolutionary subversion and attack.

One might recall how, in 1918-20, fourteen capitalist nations, including the United States, invaded Soviet Russia in a bloody but unsuccessful attempt to overthrow the revolutionary Bolshevik gov-

---

[7] Marx, Engels, Lenin, *Anarchism and Anarcho-Syndicalism: Selected Writings* (New York: International Publishers, 1972), 139. In her biography of Louise Michel, the anarchist historian Edith Thomas asserts that anarchism is "the absence of government, the direct adminstration by people of their own lives." Who could not want that? Thomas doesn't say how it would work except to assert that "anarchists want it right now, in all the confusion and disorder of right now." She notes proudly that anarchism "is still intact as an ideal, for it has never been tried." That is exactly the problem. Why in so many hundreds of actual rebellions, including ones led by anarchists themselves, has anarchism never been tried or never succeeded in surviving for any length of time in an "intact" anarchist form? (In the anarchist uprising Engels described, the rebels, in seeming violation of their own ideology, did not rely on Thomas's "direct administration by the people" but set up ruling juntas.) The unpracticed, unattainable quality of the ideal helps it to retain its better-than-anything appeal in the minds of some.

ernment. The years of foreign invasion and civil war did much to intensify the Bolsheviks' siege psychology with its commitment to lockstep party unity and a repressive security apparatus. Thus, in May 1921, the same Lenin who had encouraged the practice of internal party democracy and struggled against Trotsky in order to give the trade unions a greater measure of autonomy, now called for an end to the Workers' Opposition and other factional groups within the party.[8] "The time has come," he told an enthusiastically concurring Tenth Party Congress, "to put an end to opposition, to put a lid on it: we have had enough opposition." Open disputes and conflicting tendencies within and without the party, the communists concluded, created an appearance of division and weakness that invited attack by formidable foes.

Only a month earlier, in April 1921, Lenin had called for more worker representation on the party's Central Committee. In short, he had become not anti-worker but anti-opposition. Here was a social revolution—like every other—that was not allowed to develop its political and material life in an unhindered way.[9]

By the late 1920s, the Soviets faced the choice of (a) moving in a still more centralized direction with a command economy and forced agrarian collectivization and full-speed industrialization under a commandist, autocratic party leadership, the road taken by

---

[8] Trotsky was among the more authoritarian Bolshevik leaders, least inclined to tolerate organizational autonomy, diverse views, and internal party democracy. But in the fall of 1923, finding himself in a minority position, outmaneuvered by Stalin and others, Trotsky developed a sudden commitment to open party procedures and workers' democracy. Ever since, he has been hailed by some followers as an anti-Stalinist democrat.

[9] Regarding the several years before 1921, the Sovietologist Stephen Cohen writes, "The experience of civil war and war communism profoundly altered both the party and the emerging political system." Other socialist parties were expelled from the soviets. And the Communist party's "democratic norms . . . as well as its almost libertarian and reformist profile" gave way to a "rigid authoritarianism and pervasive 'militarization.'" Much of the popular control exercised by local soviets and factory committees was eliminated. In the words of one Bolshevik leader, "The republic is an armed camp": see Cohen's *Bukharin and the Bolshevik Revolution* (New York: Oxford University Press, 1973), 79.

Stalin, or (b) moving in a liberalized direction, allowing more political diversity, more autonomy for labor unions and other organizations, more open debate and criticism, greater autonomy among the various Soviet republics, a sector of privately owned small businesses, independent agricultural development by the peasantry, greater emphasis on consumer goods, and less effort given to the kind of capital accumulation needed to build a strong military-industrial base.

The latter course, I believe, would have produced a more comfortable, more humane and serviceable society. Siege socialism would have given way to worker-consumer socialism. The only problem is that the country would have risked being incapable of withstanding the Nazi onslaught. Instead, the Soviet Union embarked upon a rigorous, forced industrialization. This policy has often been mentioned as one of the wrongs perpetrated by Stalin upon his people.[10] It consisted mostly of building, within a decade, an entirely new, huge industrial base east of the Urals in the middle of the barren steppes, the biggest steel complex in Europe, in anticipation of an invasion from the West. "Money was spent like water, men froze, hungered and suffered but the construction went on with a disregard for individuals and a mass heroism seldom paralleled in history."[11]

Stalin's prophecy that the Soviet Union had only ten years to do what the British had done in a century proved correct. When the Nazis invaded in 1941, that same industrial base, safely ensconced thousands of miles from the front, produced the weapons of war that eventually turned the tide. The cost of this survival included 22 million Soviet citizens who perished in the war and immeasurable devastation and suffering, the effects of which would distort Soviet society for decades afterward.

---

[10] To give one of innumerable examples, recently Roger Burbach faulted Stalin for "rushing the Soviet Union headlong on the road to industrialization": see his correspondence, *Monthly Review,* March 1996, 35.

[11] John Scott, *Behind the Urals, an American Worker in Russia's City of Steel* (Boston: Houghton Mifflin, 1942).

All this is not to say that everything Stalin did was of historical necessity. The exigencies of revolutionary survival did not "make inevitable" the heartless execution of hundreds of Old Bolshevik leaders, the personality cult of a supreme leader who claimed every revolutionary gain as his own achievement, the suppression of party political life through terror, the eventual silencing of debate regarding the pace of industrialization and collectivization, the ideological regulation of all intellectual and cultural life, and the mass deportations of "suspect" nationalities.

The transforming effects of counterrevolutionary attack have been felt in other countries. A Sandinista military officer I met in Vienna in 1986 noted that Nicaraguans were "not a warrior people" but they had to learn to fight because they faced a destructive, U.S.-sponsored mercenary war. She bemoaned the fact that war and embargo forced her country to postpone much of its socio-economic agenda. As with Nicaragua, so with Mozambique, Angola and numerous other countries in which U.S.-financed mercenary forces destroyed farmlands, villages, health centers, and power stations, while killing or starving hundreds of thousands—the revolutionary baby was strangled in its crib or mercilessly bled beyond recognition. This reality ought to earn at least as much recognition as the suppression of dissidents in this or that revolutionary society.

The overthrow of Eastern European and Soviet communist governments was cheered by many left intellectuals. Now democracy would have its day. The people would be free from the yoke of communism and the U.S. Left would be free from the albatross of existing communism, or as left theorist Richard Lichtman put it, "liberated from the incubus of the Soviet Union and the succubus of Communist China."

In fact, the capitalist restoration in Eastern Europe seriously weakened the numerous Third World liberation struggles that had received aid from the Soviet Union and brought a whole new crop of right-wing governments into existence, ones that now worked hand-in-glove with U.S. global counterrevolutionaries around the globe.

In addition, the overthrow of communism gave the green light to the unbridled exploitative impulses of Western corporate interests. No longer needing to convince workers that they live better than their counterparts in Russia, and no longer restrained by a competing system, the corporate class is rolling back the many gains that working people in the West have won over the years. Now that the free market, in its meanest form, is emerging triumphant in the East, so will it prevail in the West. "Capitalism with a human face" is being replaced by "capitalism in your face." As Richard Levins put it, "So in the new exuberant aggressiveness of world capitalism we see what communists and their allies had held at bay" (*Monthly Review*, 9/96).

Having never understood the role that existing communist powers played in tempering the worst impulses of Western capitalism and imperialism, and having perceived communism as nothing but an unmitigated evil, the left anticommunists did not anticipate the losses that were to come. Some of them still don't get it.

CHAPTER 4

COMMUNISM IN WONDERLAND

The various communist countries suffered from major systemic deficiencies. While these internal problems were seriously exacerbated by the destruction and military threat imposed by the Western capitalist powers, there were a number of difficulties that seemed to inhere in the system itself.

Rewarding Inefficiency

All communist nations were burdened by rigid economic command systems.[1] Central planning was useful and even necessary in the earlier period of siege socialism to produce steel, wheat, and tanks in order to build an industrial base and withstand the Nazi onslaught. But it eventually hindered technological development and growth, and proved incapable of supplying a wide-enough range of consumer goods and services. No computerized system could be devised to accurately model a vast and intricate economy.

---

[1] While framed in the past tense, the following discussion also applies to the few remaining communist countries still in existence.

No system could gather and process the immense range of detailed information needed to make correct decisions about millions of production tasks.

Top-down planning stifled initiative throughout the system. Stagnation was evident in the failure of the Soviet industrial establishment to apply the innovations of the scientific-technological revolution of the 1970s and 1980s, including the use of computer technology. Though the Soviets produced many of the world's best mathematicians, physicists, and other scientists, little of their work found actual application. As Mikhail Gorbachev complained before the 28th Communist Party Congress in 1990, "We can no longer tolerate the managerial system that rejects scientific and technological progress and new technologies, that is committed to cost-ineffectiveness and generates squandering and waste."

It is not enough to denounce ineptitude, one must also try to explain why it persisted despite repeated exhortations from leaders—going as far back as Stalin himself who seethed about time-serving bureaucrats. An explanation for the failure of the managerial system may be found in the system itself, which created *dis*incentives for innovation:

1. Managers were little inclined to pursue technological paths that might lead to their own obsolescence. Many of them were not competent in the new technologies and should have been replaced.

2. Managers received no rewards for taking risks. They maintained their positions regardless of whether innovative technology was developed, as was true of their superiors and central planners.

3. Supplies needed for technological change were not readily available. Since inputs were fixed by the plan and all materials and labor were fully committed, it was difficult to divert resources to innovative production. In addition, experimentation increased the risks of failing to meet one's quotas.

4. There was no incentive to produce better machines for other enterprises since that brought no rewards to one's own firm. Quite

the contrary, under the pressure to get quantitative results, managers often cut corners on quality.

5. There was a scarcity of replacement parts both for industrial production and for durable-use consumer goods. Because top planners set such artificially low prices for spare parts, it was seldom cost-efficient for factories to produce them.

6. Because producers did not pay real-value prices for raw materials, fuel, and other things, enterprises often used them inefficiently.

7. Productive capacity was under-utilized. Problems of distribution led to excessive unused inventory. Because of irregular shipments, there was a tendency to hoard more than could be put into production, further adding to shortages.

8. Improvements in production would lead only to an increase in one's production quota. In effect, well-run factories were punished with greater work loads. Poor performing ones were rewarded with lower quotas and state subsidies.

Managerial irresponsibility was a problem in agriculture as well as industry. One Vietnamese farm organizer's comment could describe the situation in most other communist countries: "The painful lesson of [farm] cooperatization was that management was not motivated to succeed or produce." If anything, farm management was often motivated to provide a poor product. For instance, since state buyers of meat paid attention to quantity rather than quality, collective farmers maximized profits by producing fatter animals. Consumers might not care to eat fatty meat but that was their problem. Only a foolish or saintly farmer would work harder to produce better quality meat for the privilege of getting paid less.

As in all countries, bureaucracy tended to become a self-feeding animal. Administrative personnel increased at a faster rate than productive workers. In some enterprises, administrative personnel made up half the full number of workers. A factory with 11,000 production workers might have an administrative staff of 5,000, a considerable burden on productivity.

The heavily bureaucratic mode of operation did not allow for critical, self-corrective feedback. In general, there was a paucity of the kind of debate that might have held planners and managers accountable to the public. The fate of the whistleblower was the same in communist countries as in our own. Those who exposed waste, incompetence, and corruption were more likely to run risks than receive rewards.

Nobody Minding the Store

We have been taught that people living under communism suffer from "the totalitarian control over every aspect of life," as *Time* magazine (5/27/96) still tells us. Talking to the people themselves, one found that they complained less about overbearing control than about the *absence* of responsible control. Maintenance people failed to perform needed repairs. Occupants of a new housing project might refuse to pay rent and no one bothered to collect it. With lax management in harvesting, storage, and transportation, as much as 30 percent of all produce was lost between field and store and thousands of tons of meat were left to spoil. People complained about broken toilets, leaky roofs, rude salespeople, poor quality goods, late trains, deficient hospital services, and corrupt and unresponsive bureaucrats.

Corruption and favoritism were commonplace. There was the manager who regularly pilfered the till, the workers who filched foodstuffs and goods from state stores or supplies from factories in order to service private homes for personal gain, the peasants on collective farms who stripped parts from tractors to sell them on the black market, the director who accepted bribes to place people at the top of a waiting list to buy cars, and the farmers who hoarded livestock which they sold to townspeople at three times the government's low procurement price. All this was hardly the behavior of people trembling under a totalitarian rule of terror.

The system itself rewarded evasion and noncompliance. Thus, the poorer the performance of the collective farm, the more substantial the subsidy and the less demanded in the way of work quotas. The poorer the performance of plumbers and mechanics, the less burdened they were with calls and quotas. The poorer the restaurant service, the fewer the number of clients and the more food left over to take home for oneself or sell on the black market. The last thing restaurant personnel wanted was satisfied customers who would return to dine at the officially fixed low prices.

Not surprisingly, work discipline left much to be desired. There was the clerk who chatted endlessly with a friend on the telephone while a long line of people waited resentfully for service, the two workers who took three days to paint a hotel wall that should have taken a few hours, the many who would walk off their jobs to go shopping. Such poor performance itself contributed to low productivity and the cycle of scarcity. In 1979, Cuban leader Raul Castro offered this list of abuses:

> [The] lack of work discipline, unjustified absences from work, deliberate go-slows so as not to surpass the norms—which are already low and poorly applied in practice—so that they won't be changed. . . . In contrast to capitalism, when people in the countryside worked an exhausting 12-hour workday and more, there are a good many instances today especially in agriculture, of people . . . working no more than four or six hours, with the exception of canecutters and possibly a few other kinds of work. We know that in many cases heads of brigades and foremen make a deal with workers to meet the norm in half a day and then go off and work for the other half for some nearby small [private] farmer [for extra income]; or to go slow and meet the norm in seven or eight hours; or do two or three norms in a day and report them over other days on which they don't go to work. . . .
>
> All these "tricks of the trade" in agriculture are also to be found in industry, transportation services, repair shops and many other places where there's rampant buddyism, cases of "you do me a favor and I'll do you one" and pilfering on the side. (*Cuba Update,* 3/80)

If fired, an individual had a constitutional guarantee to another job and seldom had any difficulty finding one. The labor market was a seller's market. Workers did not fear losing their jobs but managers feared losing their best workers and sometimes overpaid them to prevent them from leaving. Too often, however, neither monetary rewards nor employment itself were linked to performance. The dedicated employee usually earned no more than the irresponsible one. The slackers and pilferers had a demoralizing effect on those who wanted to work in earnest.

Full employment was achieved by padding the workforce with people who had relatively little to do. This added to labor scarcity, low productivity, lack of work discipline, and the failure to implement labor-saving technologies that could maximize production.

The communists operated on the assumption that once capitalism and its attendant economic abuses were eliminated, and once social production was communalized and people were afforded some decent measure of security and prosperity, they would contentedly do their fair share of work. That often proved not so.

Communist economies had a kind of Wonderland quality in that prices seldom bore any relation to actual cost or value. Many expensive services were provided almost entirely free, such as education, medical care, and most recreational, sporting, and cultural events. Housing, transportation, utilities, and basic foods were heavily subsidized. Many people had money but not much to buy with it. High-priced quality goods and luxury items were hard to come by. All this in turn affected work performance. Why work hard to earn more when there was not that much to buy?

Wage increases, designed to attract workers to disagreeable or low-prestige jobs or as incentives to production, only added to the disparity between purchasing power and the supply of goods. Prices were held artificially low, first out of dedication to egalitarian principles but also because attempts to readjust them provoked worker protests in Poland, East Germany, and the USSR. Thus in the Soviet

Union and Poland, the state refused to raise the price of bread, which was priced at only a few pennies per loaf, though it cost less than animal feed. One result: Farmers in both countries bought the bread to feed their pigs. With rigorous price controls, there was hidden inflation, a large black market, and long shopping lines.

Citizens were expected to play by the rules and not take advantage of the system, even when the system inadvertently invited transgressions. They were expected to discard a self-interested mode of behavior when in fact there was no reward and some disadvantage in doing so. The "brutal totalitarian regime" was actually a giant trough from which many took whatever they could.

There was strong resentment concerning consumer scarcities: the endless shopping lines, the ten-year wait for a new automobile, the housing shortage that compelled single people to live at home or get married in order to qualify for an apartment of their own, and the five-year wait for that apartment. The crowding and financial dependency on parents often led to early divorce. These and other such problems took their toll on people's commitment to socialism.

Wanting It All

I listened to an East German friend complain of poor services and inferior products; the system did not work, he concluded. But what of the numerous social benefits so lacking in much of the world, I asked, aren't these to be valued? His response was revealing: "Oh, nobody ever talks about that." People took for granted what they had in the way of human services and entitlements while hungering for the consumer goods dangling in their imaginations.

The human capacity for discontent should not be underestimated. People cannot live on the social wage alone. Once our needs are satisfied, then our wants tend to escalate, and our wants become our needs. A rise in living standards often incites a still greater rise in expectations. As people are treated better, they want more of the good things and are not necessarily grateful for what they already have. Leading professionals who had attained relatively good living standards wanted to dress better, travel abroad, and enjoy the more abundant life styles available to people of means in the capitalist world.

It was this desire for greater affluence rather than the quest for political freedom that motivated most of those who emigrated to the West. Material wants were mentioned far more often than the lack of democracy. The emigrés who fled Vietnam in 1989 were not persecuted political dissidents. Usually they were relatively prosperous craftsmen, small entrepreneurs, well-educated engineers, architects, and intellectuals seeking greater opportunities. To quote one: "I don't think my life here in Vietnam is very bad. In fact, I'm very well off. But that's human nature to always want something better." Another testified: "We had two shops and our income was decent but we wanted a better life." And another: "They left for the same reasons we did. They wanted to be richer, just like us."[2] Today a "get rich" mania is spreading throughout much of Vietnam, as that nation lurches toward a market economy (*New York Times*, 4/5/96).

Likewise, the big demand in the German Democratic Republic (GDR) was for travel, new appliances, and bigger apartments (*Washington Post*, 8/28/89). The *New York Times* (3/13/90) described East Germany as a "country of 16 million [who] seem transfixed by one issue: How soon can they become as prosperous as West Germany?" A national poll taken in China reported that 68 percent chose as their goal "to live well and get rich" (PBS-TV report, 6/96).

In 1989, I asked the GDR ambassador in Washington, D.C. why his country made such junky two-cylinder cars. He said the goal was to develop good public transportation and discourage the use of costly private vehicles. But when asked to choose between a rational, efficient, economically sound and ecologically sane mass transporta-

---

[2] All quotations from the *Washington Post*, 4/12/89.

tion system or an automobile with its instant mobility, special status, privacy, and personal empowerment, the East Germans went for the latter, as do most people in the world. The ambassador added ruefully: "We thought building a good society would make good people. That's not always true." Whether or not it was a good society, at least he was belatedly recognizing the discrepancy between public ideology and private desire.

In Cuba today many youth see no value in joining the Communist party and think Fidel Castro has had his day and should step aside. The revolutionary accomplishments in education and medical care are something they take for granted and cannot get excited about. Generally they are more concerned about their own personal future than about socialism. University courses on Marxism and courses on the Cuban Revolution, once overenrolled, now go sparsely attended, while students crowd into classes on global markets and property law (*Newsday*, 4/12/96).

With the U.S. blockade and the loss of Soviet aid, the promise of abundance receded beyond sight in Cuba and the cornucopia of the North appeared ever more alluring. Many Cuban youth idealize life in the United States and long for its latest styles and music. Like the Eastern Europeans, they think capitalism will deliver the goodies at no special cost. When told that young people in the United States face serious hurdles, they respond with all the certainty of inexperience: "We know that many people in the States are poor and that many are rich. If you work hard, however, you can do well. It is the land of opportunity" (*Monthly Review*, 4/96).

By the second or third generation, relatively few are still alive who can favorably contrast their lives under socialism with the great hardships and injustices of prerevolutionary days. As stated by one Cuban youth who has no memory of life before the revolution: "We're tired of the slogans. That was all right for our parents but the revolution is history" (*San Francisco Chronicle*, 8/25/95).

In a society of rapidly rising—and sometimes unrealistic—expectations, those who did not do well, who could not find employment commensurate with their training, or who were stuck with drudge work, were especially inclined to want a change. Even in the best of societies, much labor has an instrumental value but no inherent gratification. The sooner a tedious task is completed, the sooner there is another to be done, so why knock yourself out? If "building the revolution" and "winning the battle of production" mean performing essential but routine tasks for the rest of one's foreseeable future, the revolution understandably loses its luster. There is often not enough interesting and creative work to go around for all who consider themselves interesting and creative people.

In time, the revolution suffers from the routinization of charisma. Ordinary people cannot sustain in everyday life a level of intense dedication for abstract albeit beautiful ideals. Why struggle for a better life if it cannot now be attained? And if it can be enjoyed now, then forget about revolutionary sacrifice.

Reactionism to the Surface

For years I heard about the devilishly clever manipulations of communist propaganda. Later on, I was surprised to discover that news media in communist countries were usually lackluster and plodding. Western capitalist nations are immersed in an advertising culture, with billions spent on marketing and manipulating images. The communist countries had nothing comparable. Their media coverage generally consisted of dull protocol visits and official pronouncements, along with glowing reports about the economy and society—so glowing that people complained about not knowing what was going on in their own country. They could read about abuses of power, industrial accidents, worker protests, and earthquakes occurring in every country but their own. And even when the press exposed domestic abuses, they usually went uncorrected.

Media reports sometimes so conflicted with daily experience that the official press was not believed even when it did tell the truth, as when it reported on poverty and repression in the capitalist world. If anything, many intellectuals in communist nations were utterly starry-eyed about the capitalist world and unwilling to look at its seamier side. Ferociously opposed to the socialist system, they were anticommunist to the point of being full-fledged adulators of Western reactionism. The more rabidly "reactionary chic" a position was, the more appeal it had for the intelligentsia.

With almost religious fervor, intellectuals maintained that the capitalist West, especially the United States, was a free-market paradise of superabundance and almost limitless opportunity. Nor would they believe anything to the contrary. With complete certitude, well-fed, university-educated, Moscow intellectuals sitting in their modest but comfortable apartments would tell U.S. visitors, "The poorest among you live better than we."

A conservative deputy editor of the *Wall Street Journal*, David Brooks, offers this profile of the Moscow intellectual:

> He is the master of contempt, and feels he is living in a world run by imbeciles. He is not unsure, casting about for the correct answers. The immediate answers are obvious — democracy and capitalism. His self-imposed task is to smash the idiots who stand in the way. . . . He has none of the rococo mannerisms of our intellectuals, but values bluntness, rudeness, and arrogance. . . . [These] democratic intellectuals [love] Ronald Reagan, Marlboros, and the South in the American Civil War. (*National Review,* 3/2/92)

Consider Andrei Sakharov, a darling of the U.S. press, who regularly praised corporate capitalism while belittling the advances achieved by the Soviet people. He lambasted the U.S. peace movement for its opposition to the Vietnam War and accused the Soviets of being military expansionists and the sole culprits behind the arms race. Sakharov supported every U.S. armed intervention abroad as a defense of democracy and characterized new U.S. weapons systems like the neutron bomb as "primarily defensive." Anointed by U.S.

leaders and media as a "human rights advocate," he never had an unkind word for the human rights violations perpetrated by the fascist regimes of faithful U.S. client states, including Pinochet's Chile and Suharto's Indonesia, and he directed snide remarks toward those who did. He regularly attacked those in the West who dissented from anticommunist orthodoxy and who opposed U.S. interventionism abroad. As with many other Eastern European intellectuals, Sakharov's advocacy of dissent did not extend to opinions that deviated to the left of his own.[3]

The tolerance for Western imperialism extended into the upper reaches of the Soviet government itself, as reflected in a remark made in 1989 by a high-ranking official in the Soviet Foreign Ministry, Andrey Kozyrev, who stated that Third World countries "suffer not so much from capitalism as from a lack of it." Either by design or stupidity he confused capital (which those nations lack) with capitalism (of which they have more than enough to victimize them). He also claimed that "none of the main [bourgeois groups] in America are connected with militarism." To think of them as imperialists who plunder Third World countries is a "stereotyped idea" that should be discarded (*New York Times*, 1/7/89).

As a system of analysis mainly concerned with existing capitalism, Marxism has relatively little to say about the development of socialist societies. In the communist countries, Marxism was doled out

---

[3] See Andrei Sakharov, *My Country and the World* (New York: Vintage Books, 1975), especially chapters 3, 4, and 5. A memorable moment was provided me by the noted journalist I.F. Stone, in Washington, D.C. in 1987. Izzy (as he was called) had just given a talk at the Institute for Policy Studies praising Sakharov as a courageous champion of democracy, a portrayal that seemed heavily indebted to the U.S. media image of Sakharov. Encountering Stone in the street after the event, I said to him that we should distinguish between Sakharov's right to speak, which I supported, and the reactionary, CIA-ridden content of his speech, which we were under no obligation to admire. He stopped me in mid-sentence and screamed: "I'm sick and tired of people who wipe the ass of the Soviet Union!" He then stomped away. Izzy Stone was normally a polite man, but as with many on the U.S. Left, his anti-Sovietism could cause him to discard both rational discourse and common courtesy. On subsequent occasions he talked to me in a most friendly manner but never once thought to apologize for that outburst.

like a catechism. Its critique of capitalism had no vibrancy or meaning for those who lived in a noncapitalist society. Instead, most intellectuals found excitement in the forbidden fruit of Western bourgeois ideology. In looking to the West, they were not interested in broadening the ideological spectrum, a desirable goal, but in replacing the dominant view with a rightist anticommunist orthodoxy. They were not for an end to ideology but for replacing one ideology with another. Without hesitation, they added their voices to the chorus singing the glories of the free-market paradise.

Heavily subsidized by Western sources, the right-wing intelligentsia produced publications like *Moscow News* and *Argumentyi Fakti* which put out a virulently pro-capitalist, pro-imperialist message. One such publication, *Literaturnaya Gazeta* (March 1990), hailed Reagan and Bush as "statesmen" and "the architects of peace." It questioned the need for a Ministry of Culture in the USSR, even one that was now headed by an anticommunist: "There is no such ministry in the United States and yet it seems that there is nothing wrong with American culture." Who said Russians don't have a sense of humor?

With the decline of communist power in Eastern Europe, the worst political scum began to float to the surface, Nazi sympathizers and hate groups of all sorts, though they were not the only purveyors of bigotry. In 1990, none other than Polish Solidarity leader Lech Walesa declared that "a gang of Jews had gotten hold of the trough and is bent on destroying us." Later on he maintained that the comment did not apply to all Jews but only those "who are looking out for themselves while giving not a damn about anyone else" (*Nation,* 9/10/90). The following year, in Poland's post-communist presidential election, various candidates (including Walesa) outdid each other in their anti-Semitic allusions. In 1996, at a national ceremony, Solidarity chief Zygmunt Wrzodak resorted to anti-Semitic vituperation while railing against the previous communist regime (*New York Times,* 7/9/96).

Romanticizing Capitalism

In 1990, in Washington, D.C., the Hungarian ambassador held a press conference to announce that his country was discarding its socialist system because it did not work. When I asked why it did not work, he said, "I don't know." Here was someone who confessed that he had no understanding of the deficiencies of his country's socio-economic process, even though he was one of those in charge of that process. Leaders who talk only to each other are soon out of touch with reality.

The policymakers of these communist states showed a surprisingly un-Marxist understanding of the problems they faced. There were denunciations and admonitions aplenty, but little systemic analysis of why and how things had come to such an impasse. Instead, there was much admiration for what was taken to be Western capitalist know-how and remarkably little understanding of the uglier side of capitalism and how it impacted upon the world.

In the USSR, glasnost (the use of critical debate to invite innovation and reform) opened Soviet media to Western penetration, and accelerated the very disaffection it was intended to rectify. Leaders in Poland and Hungary, and eventually the Soviet Union and the other European communist nations, decided to open their economies to Western investment during the late 1980s. It was anticipated that state ownership would exist on equal terms with cooperatives, foreign investors, and domestic private entrepreneurs (*Washington Post*, 4/17/89). In fact, the whole state economy was put at risk and eventually undermined. Communist leaders had even less understanding of the capitalist system than of their own.

Most people living under socialism had little understanding of capitalism in practice. Workers interviewed in Poland believed that if their factory were to be closed down in the transition to the free market, "the state will find us some other work" (*New Yorker*, 11/13/89). They thought they would have it both ways. In the Soviet Union, many who argued for privatization also expected the government to continue providing them with collective benefits and subsidies. One skeptical farmer got it right: "Some people want to be capitalists for themselves, but expect socialism to keep serving them" (*Guardian,* 10/23/91).

Reality sometimes hit home. In 1990, during the glasnost period, when the Soviet government announced that the price of newsprint would be raised 300 percent to make it commensurate with its actual cost, the new procapitalist publications complained bitterly. They were angry that state socialism would no longer subsidize their denunciations of state socialism. They were being subjected to the same free-market realities they so enthusiastically advocated for everyone else, and they did not like it.

Not everyone romanticized capitalism. Many of the Soviet and Eastern European emigrés who had migrated to the United States during the 1970s and 1980s complained about this country's poor social services, crime, harsh work conditions, lack of communitarian spirit, vulgar electoral campaigns, inferior educational standards, and the astonishing ignorance that Americans had about history.

They discovered they could no longer leave their jobs during the day to go shopping, that their employers provided no company doctor when they fell ill on the job, that they were subject to severe reprimands when tardy, that they could not walk the streets and parks late at night without fear, that they might not be able to afford medical services for their family or college tuition for their children, and that they had no guarantee of a job and might experience unemployment at any time.

Among those who never emigrated were some who did not harbor illusions about capitalism. In fact, numerous workers, peasants, and elderly were fearful of the changes ahead and not entirely sold on the free-market mythology. A 1989 survey in Czechoslovakia found that 47 percent wanted their economy to remain state controlled, while 43 percent wanted a mixed economy, and only 3 percent said they favored capitalism (*New York Times,* 12/1/89). In May 1991, a

survey of Russians by a U.S. polling organization found that 54 percent chose some form of socialism and only 20 percent wanted a
free-market economy such as in the United States or Germany.
Another 27 percent elected for "a modified form of capitalism as
found in Sweden" (*Monthly Review*, 12/94).

Still, substantial numbers, especially among intellectuals and
youths—the two groups who know everything—opted for the free-
market paradise, without the faintest notion of its social costs.
Against the inflated imagination, reality is a poor thing. Against the
glittering image of the West's cornucopia, the routinized, scarcity-
ridden, and often exasperating experiences of communist society did
not have a chance.

It seems communism created a dialectical dynamic that undermined itself. It took semi-feudal, devastated, underdeveloped countries and successfully industrialized them, bringing a better life for
most. But this very process of modernization and uplift also created
expectations that could not be fulfilled. Many expected to keep all
the securities of socialism, overlaid with capitalist consumerism. As
we shall see in subsequent chapters, they were in for some painful
surprises.

One reason siege socialism could not make the transition to consumer socialism is that the state of siege was never lifted. As noted in
the previous chapter, the very real internal deficiencies within communist systems were exacerbated by unrelenting external attacks and
threats from the Western powers. Born into a powerfully hostile capitalist world, communist nations suffered through wars, invasions,
and an arms race that exhausted their productive capacities and
retarded their development. The decision by Soviet leaders to achieve
military parity with the United States—while working from a much
smaller industrial base—placed a serious strain on the entire Soviet
economy.

The very siege socialism that allowed the USSR to survive made
it difficult for it to thrive. Perestroika (the restructuring of socio-

economic practices in order to improve performance) was intended to open and revitalize production. Instead it led to the unraveling of the entire state socialist fabric. Thus the pluralistic media that were to replace the communist monopoly media eventually devolved into a procapitalist ideological monopoly. The same thing happened to other socialist institutions. The intent was to use a shot of capitalism to bolster socialism; the reality was that socialism was used to subsidize and build an unforgiving capitalism.

Pressed hard throughout its history by global capitalism's powerful financial, economic, and military forces, state socialism endured a perpetually tenuous existence, only to be swept away when the floodgates were opened to the West.

CHAPTER 5

STALIN'S FINGERS

In 1989-1991, remarkable transformations swept across Eastern Europe and the Soviet Union. Communist governments were overthrown, large portions of their publicly owned economies were dismantled and handed over to private owners at garage sale prices. And one-party rule was replaced with multi-party parliamentary systems. For Western leaders, who had tirelessly pursued the rollback of communism, it was a dream come true.

If the overthrow of communism was a victory for democracy, as some claimed, it was even more a victory for free-market capitalism and conservative anticommunism. Some of the credit should go to the CIA and other cold war agencies, along with the National Endowment for Democracy, the AFL-CIO, the Ford Foundation, the Rockefeller Brothers Fund, the Pew Charitable Trusts, and various right-wing groups, all of whom funded free-market, anticommunist political organizations and publications throughout Eastern Europe and the Soviet Union, in what swiftly became the best financed chain of "revolutions" in history.

The upheavals occurred with remarkably little violence. As Lech Walesa boasted in November 1989, Polish Solidarity overthrew the communist government without breaking a single window. This says at least as much about the government that was overthrown as about the rebels. Rather than acting as might U.S.-supported rulers in El Salvador, Colombia, Zaire, or Indonesia—with death-squad terrorism and mass repression—the communists relinquished power almost without firing a shot. The relatively peaceful transition does not fit our image of unscrupulous totalitarians who stop at nothing to maintain power over captive populations. Why didn't the ruthless Reds act more ruthlessly?[1]

How Many Victims?

We have heard much about the ruthless Reds, beginning with the reign of terror and repression perpetrated during the dictatorship of Joseph Stalin (1929-1953). Estimates of those who perished under Stalin's rule—based principally on speculations by writers who never reveal how they arrive at such figures—vary wildly. Thus, Roy Medvedev puts Stalin's victims at 5 to 7 million; Robert Conquest decided on 7 to 8 million; Olga Shatunovskaia claims 19.8 million just for the 1935-40 period; Stephen Cohen says 9 million by 1939, with 3 million executed or dying from mistreatment during the 1936-39 period; and Arthur Koestler tells us it was 20 to 25 million. More recently, William Rusher, of the Claremont Institute, refers to the "100 million people wantonly murdered by Communist dictators since the Bolshevik Revolution in 1917" (*Oakland Tribune,* 1/22/96) and Richard Lourie blames the Stalin era for "the slaughter of millions" (*New York Times,* 8/4/96).

---

[1] During the mid-1980s, the police in communist Poland shot forty-four demonstrators in Gdansk and other cities. Ten former police and army officers were put on trial in 1996 for these killings. In Rumania, there reportedly were scores of fatalities in the disturbances immediately preceeding the overthrow of Ceaucescu, after which Ceaucescu and his wife were summarily executed without trial. The killings in Poland and Rumania are the sum total of fatalities, as far as I know.

Unburdened by any documentation, these "estimates" invite us to conclude that the sum total of people incarcerated in the labor camps over a twenty-two year period (allowing for turnovers due to death and term expirations) would have constituted an astonishing portion of the Soviet population. The support and supervision of the gulag (all the labor camps, labor colonies, and prisons of the Soviet system) would have been the USSR's single largest enterprise.

In the absence of reliable evidence, we are fed anecdotes, such as the story Winston Churchill tells of the time he asked Stalin how many people died in the famine. According to Churchill, the Soviet leader responded by raising both his hands, a gesture that may have signified an unwillingness to broach the subject. But since Stalin happened to have five fingers on each hand, Churchill concluded — without benefit of a clarifying follow-up question — that Stalin was confessing to ten million victims. Would the head of one state (especially the secretive Stalin) casually proffer such an admission to the head of another? To this day, Western writers treat this woolly tale as an ironclad confession of mass atrocities.[2]

What we do know of Stalin's purges is that many victims were Communist party officials, managers, military officers, and other strategically situated individuals whom the dictator saw fit to incarcerate or liquidate. In addition, whole catagories of people whom Stalin considered of unreliable loyalty — Cossacks, Crimean Tarters, and ethnic Germans — were selected for internal deportation. Though they never saw the inside of a prison or labor camp, they were subjected to noncustodial resettlement in Central Asia and Siberia.

To be sure, crimes of state were committed in communist countries and many political prisoners were unjustly interned and even murdered. But the inflated numbers offered by cold-war scholars

---

[2] Stalin "confided the figure of 10 million to Winston Churchill": Stephen Cohen, *Bukharin and the Bolshevik Revolution* (New York: A.A. Knopf, 1973), 463n. No doubt, the famines that occurred during the years of Western invasion, counterrevolutionary intervention, White Guard civil war, and landowner resistance to collectivization took many victims.

serve neither historical truth nor the cause of justice but merely help to reinforce a knee-jerk fear and loathing of those terrible Reds.

In 1993, for the first time, several historians gained access to previously secret Soviet police archives and were able to establish well-documented estimates of prison and labor camp populations. They found that the total population of the entire gulag as of January 1939, near the end of the Great Purges, was 2,022,976.[3] At about that time, there began a purge of the purgers, including many intelligence and secret police (NKVD) officials and members of the judiciary and other investigative committees, who were suddenly held responsible for the excesses of the terror despite their protestations of fidelity to the regime.[4]

Soviet labor camps were not death camps like those the Nazis built across Europe. There was no systematic extermination of inmates, no gas chambers or crematoria to dispose of millions of bodies. Despite harsh conditions, the great majority of gulag inmates survived and eventually returned to society when granted amnesty or when their terms were finished. In any given year, 20 to 40 percent of the inmates were released, according to archive records.[5] Oblivious to these facts, the Moscow correspondent of the *New York Times* (7/31/96) continues to describe the gulag as "the largest system of death camps in modern history."

Almost a million gulag prisoners were released during World War II to serve in the military. The archives reveal that more than half of all gulag deaths for the 1934-53 period occurred during the war years (1941-45), mostly from malnutrition, when severe privation was the

---

[3] By way of comparison, in 1995, according to the Bureau of Justice Statistics, in the United States there were 1.6 million in prison, three million on probation, and 700,000 on parole, for a total of 5.3 million under correctional supervision (*San Francisco Chronicle,* 7/1/96). Some millions of others have served time but are no longer connected to the custodial system in any way.

[4] J. Arch Getty, Gabor Rittersporn, and Victor Zemskov, "Victims of the Soviet Penal System in the Pre-War Years: A First Approach on the Basis of Archival Evidence," *American Historical Review,* 98 (October 1993) 1017-1049.

[5] Getty, et al., "Victims of the Soviet Penal System . . ."

common lot of the entire Soviet population. (Some 22 million Soviet citizens perished in the war.) In 1944, for instance, the labor-camp death rate was 92 per 1000. By 1953, with the postwar recovery, camp deaths had declined to 3 per 1000.[6]

Should all gulag inmates be considered innocent victims of Red repression? Contrary to what we have been led to believe, those arrested for political crimes ("counterrevolutionary offenses") numbered from 12 to 33 percent of the prison population, varying from year to year. The vast majority of inmates were charged with nonpolitical offenses: murder, assault, theft, banditry, smuggling, swindling, and other violations punishable in any society.[7]

Total executions from 1921 to 1953, a thirty-three year span inclusive, were 799,455. No breakdown of this figure was provided by the researchers. It includes those who were guilty of nonpolitical capital crimes, as well as those who collaborated in the Western capitalist invasion and subsequent White Guard Army atrocities. It also includes some of the considerable numbers who collaborated with the Nazis during World War II and probably German SS prisoners. In any case, the killings of political opponents were not in the millions or tens of millions — which is not to say that the actual number was either inconsequential or justifiable.

The three historians who studied the heretofore secret gulag records concluded that the number of victims were far less than usually claimed in the West. This finding is ridiculed by anticommunist liberal Adam Hochschild, who prefers to repeat Churchill's story about Stalin's fingers (*New York Times*, 5/8/96). Like many others, Hochschild has no trouble accepting *un*documented speculations about the gulag but much difficulty accepting the documented figures drawn from NKVD archives.

---

[6] Ibid.
[7] Ibid.

Where Did the Gulag Go?

Some Russian anticommunist writers such as Solzhenitsyn and Sakharov, and many U.S. anticommunist liberals, maintain that the gulag existed right down to the last days of communism.[8] If so, where did it disappear to? After Stalin's death in 1953, more than half of the gulag inmates were freed, according to the study of the NKVD files previously cited. But if so many others remained incarcerated, why have they not materialized? When the communist states were overthrown, where were the half-starved hordes pouring out of the internment camps with their tales of travail?

One of the last remaining Soviet labor camps, Perm 35, was visited in 1989 by Republican congressmen and again in 1990 by French journalists (see *Washington Post*, 11/28/89 and *National Geographic*, 3/90, respectively). Both parties found only a few dozen prisoners, some of whom were identified as outright spies. Others were "refuseniks" who had been denied the right to emigrate. Prisoners worked eight hours a day, six days a week, for 250 rubles ($40) a month.

What of the supposedly vast numbers of political prisoners said to exist in the other "communist totalitarian police states" of Eastern Europe? Why no evidence of their mass release in the postcommunist era? And where are the mass of political prisoners in Cuba? Asked about this, Professor Alberto Prieto of the University of Havana pointed out that even a recent State Department report on human rights showed hundreds of people being tortured, killed, or

---

[8] The term "gulag" was incorporated into the English language in part because constant references were made to its presumed continued existence. A senior fellow at the liberal-oriented Institute for Policy Studies, Robert Borsage, sent me a note in December 1982, emphatically stating in part that "the gulag exists." When I gave talks at college campuses during the 1980s about President Reagan's domestic spending policies, I repeatedly encountered faculty members who regardless of the topic under discussion insisted that I also talk about the gulag which, they said, still contained many millions of victims. My refusal to genuflect to that orthodoxy upset a number of them.

"disappeared" in almost all the Latin American countries, but mentions only six alleged political prisoners in reference to Cuba (*People's Weekly World*, 2/26/94).

If there were mass atrocities right down to the last days of communism, why did not the newly installed anticommunist regimes seize the opportunity to bring erstwhile communist rulers to justice? Why no Nuremberg-style public trials documenting widespread atrocities? Why were not hundreds of party leaders and security officials and thousands of camp guards rounded up and tried for the millions they supposedly exterminated? The best the West Germans could do was charge East German leader Erich Honecker, several other officials, and seven border guards with shooting people who tried to escape over the Berlin Wall, a serious charge but hardly indicative of a gulag.

Authorities in the Western capitalist Federal Republic of Germany (FRG) did contrive a charge of "treason" against persons who served as officials, military officers, soldiers, judges, attorneys, and others of the now-defunct German Democratic Republic (GDR), a sovereign nation that once had full standing in the United Nations, and most of whose citizens had never been subjects of the FRG. As of 1996, more than three hundred "treason" cases had been brought to trial, including a former GDR intelligence chief, a defense minister, and six generals, all indicted for carrying out what were their legal duties under the constitution and laws of the GDR, in some instances fighting fascism and CIA sabotage. Many of the defendants were eventually acquitted but a number were sentenced to prison. What we witness here is the Nuremberg trials in reverse: Reds put on trial for their anti-fascist efforts by West German friendly-to-fascism prosecutors, using a retroactive application of FRG penal law for GDR citizens. As of the beginning of 1997, several thousand more trials were expected.[9]

---

[9] The vice-president of the highest court in the GDR, was a man named Reinwarth, who had been put in a concentration camp by the Nazis during the war and who

In 1995, Miroslav Stephan, the former secretary of the Prague Communist party, was sentenced to two and a half years for ordering Czech police to use tear gas and water cannons against demonstrators in 1988. Is this the best example of bloodthirsty Red oppression that the capitalist restorationists in Czechoslovakia could find? An action that does not even qualify as a crime in most Western nations?

In 1996 in Poland, twelve elderly Stalin-era political policemen were sentenced to prison for having beaten and mistreated prisoners—over fifty years earlier—during the communist takeover after World War II (*San Francisco Chronicle*, 3/9/96). Again one might wonder why post-communist leaders seeking to bring the communist tyrants to justice could find nothing more serious to prosecute than a police assault case from a half-century before.

Most of those incarcerated in the gulag were not political prisoners, and the same appears to be true of inmates in the other communist states. In 1989, when the millionaire playwright Vaclav Havel became president of Czechoslovakia, he granted amnesty to about two-thirds of the country's prison population, which numbered not in the millions but in the thousands. Havel assumed that most of those incarcerated under communism were victims of political repression and therefore deserved release. He and his associates were dismayed to discover that a good number were experienced crimi-

was the presiding judge in trials that convicted several CIA agents for sabotage. He was sentenced in 1996 to three-and-a-half years. Helene Heymann, who had been imprisoned during the Hitler regime for her anti-Nazi activities, later was a judge in the GDR, where she presided over anti-sabotage trials. She was put on trial in 1996. When her conviction was read out, it was pointed out by the judge that an additional factor against her was that she was trained by a Jewish lawyer who had been a defense attorney for the Communists and Social Democrats. Also put on trial were GDR soldiers who served as border guards. More than twenty GDR soldiers were shot to death from the Western side in various incidents that went unreported in the Western press: Klaus Fiske, "Witchhunt Trials of East German Leaders Continue," *People's Weekly World*, 10/19/96. These trials are in direct violation of the FRG/GDR Unification Treaty, which states that any criminal prosecution of acts undertaken in the GDR is to be done in accordance with GDR laws operative at the time.

nals who lost no time in resuming their unsavory pursuits (*New York Times,* 12/18/91).

Memories of Maldevelopment

In chapter two I discussed the role of popular revolution in advancing the condition of humankind. That analysis would apply as well to communist revolutions and is worth reiterating in the present context. We hear a great deal about the crimes of communism but almost nothing about its achievements. The communist governments inherited societies burdened with an age-old legacy of economic exploitation and maldevelopment. Much of precommunist Eastern Europe, as with prerevolutionary Russia and China, was in effect a Third World region with widespread poverty and almost nonexistent capital formation. Most rural transportation was still by horse and wagon.

The devastation of World War II added another heavy layer of misery upon the region, reducing hundreds of villages and many cities to rubble. It was the communists and their allies who rebuilt these societies. While denounced in the U.S. press for leaving their economies in bad shape, in fact, the Reds left the economy of Eastern Europe in far better condition than they found it.

The same was true of China. Henry Rosemont, Jr. notes that when the communists liberated Shanghai from the U.S.-supported reactionary Kuomintang regime in 1949, about 20 percent of that city's population, an estimated 1.2 million, were drug addicts. Every morning there were special street crews "whose sole task was to gather up the corpses of the children, adults, and the elderly who had been murdered during the night, or had been abandoned, and died of disease, cold, and/or starvation" (*Z Magazine,* October 1995).

During the years of Stalin's reign, the Soviet nation made dramatic gains in literacy, industrial wages, health care, and women's rights. These accomplishments usually go unmentioned when the

Stalinist era is discussed. To say that "socialism doesn't work" is to overlook the fact that it did. In Eastern Europe, Russia, China, Mongolia, North Korea, and Cuba, revolutionary communism created a life for the mass of people that was far better than the wretched existence they had endured under feudal lords, military bosses, foreign colonizers, and Western capitalists. The end result was a dramatic improvement in living conditions for hundreds of millions of people on a scale never before or since witnessed in history.

State socialism transformed desperately poor countries into modernized societies in which everyone had enough food, clothing, and shelter; where elderly people had secure pensions; and where all children (and many adults) went to school and no one was denied medical attention. Some of us from poor families who carry around the hidden injuries of class are much impressed by these achievements and are unwilling to dismiss them as merely "economistic."

But what of the democratic rights that these peoples were denied? In fact, with the exception of Czechoslovakia, these countries had known little political democracy in the days before communism. Russia was a czarist autocracy, Poland a rightist dictatorship with concentration camps of its own, Albania an Italian fascist protectorate as early as 1927, Cuba a U.S.-sponsored dictatorship. Lithuania, Hungary, Rumania, and Bulgaria were outright fascist regimes allied with Nazi Germany in World War II.

Then there were the distorting effects that unremitting capitalist encirclement had upon the building of socialism. Throughout its entire seventy-three-year history of counterrevolutionary invasion, civil war, forced industrialization, Stalinist purges and deportations, Nazi conquest, cold war, and nuclear arms race, the Soviet Union did not know one day of peaceful development. In the attempt to maintain military parity with the United States, the Soviets took on crushing defense costs that seriously depleted their civilian economy. In addition, they faced monetary boycott, trade discrimination, and technological embargo from the West. The people who lived under communism endured chronic shortages, long lines, poor quality goods and services, and many other problems. They wanted a better life, and who could blame them? Without capitalist encirclement, they would have had a better chance of solving more of their internal problems.

All this is not to deny the very real deficiencies of the communist systems. Here I want to point out that much of the credit for the deformation and overthrow of communism should go to the Western forces that tirelessly dedicated themselves to that task, using every possible means of political, economic, military, and diplomatic aggression to achieve a success that will continue to cost the people of the world dearly.

CHAPTER 6

THE FREE-MARKET PARADISE
GOES EAST (I)

Capitalist restoration in the former communist countries has taken different forms. In Eastern Europe and the Soviet Union, it involved the overthrow of communist governments. In China, it proceeded within the framework of a communist system—as seems to be happening in Vietnam, and perhaps will happen eventually in North Korea and Cuba. While the Chinese government continues under a nominally communist leadership, the process of private capital penetration goes on more or less unhindered.

Suppression of the Left

The anticommunists who took power in Eastern Europe and the Soviet Union in 1989-91 set about to impose bourgeois dominance over political and cultural life, purging communists from government, the media, universities, professions, and courts. While presenting themselves as democratic reformers, they soon grew impatient with the way democratic forms of popular resistance limited their efforts to install an unrestrained free-market capitalism.

In Russia, associates of President Boris Yeltsin talked of the "dangers of democracy" and complained that "most representative bodies have become a hindrance to our [market] reforms." (*Nation*, 12/2/91 and 5/4/92). Apparently, the free market, said by "reformers" to be the very foundation of political democracy, could not be introduced through democratic means. In 1992, the presidents of Poland, Czechoslovakia, and Russia demanded that their parliaments be suspended and they be allowed to rule by presidential decree, with repressive measures against "hardliners" and "holdovers" who resisted the free-market "reforms." Their goal was not power to the people but profits to the privileged.

This process of democratization-via-suppression began even before the actual overthrow of communism. In 1991, Soviet president Mikhail Gorbachev, prodded by Russian president Yeltsin, announced that the Communist party of the USSR no longer had legal status. The party's membership funds and buildings were confiscated. Workers were prohibited from engaging in any kind of political activities in the workplace. Six leftist newspapers were suppressed, while all other publications, many of them openly reactionary, enjoyed uninterrupted distribution. The U.S. media, and even many on the U.S. Left, hailed these acts of suppression as "moving ahead with democratic reforms."

Gorbachev then demanded that the Soviet Congress abolish itself. It had remained too resistant to change. Actually the Congress was not opposed to democratic debate and multi-party elections; these were already in practice. It resisted an unbridled free-market capitalism, and for that reason would have to go. Gorbachev repeatedly cut off the microphones during debate and threatened singlehandedly to abolish the Congress by emergency decree. He forced a vote three times until he got the desired abolition. These strong-arm methods were reported in the U.S. press without critical comment.

What gave Yeltsin and Gorbachev the excuse to pursue this repressive course was the curious incident of August 1991, when a nervous group of leaders, mouthing vague phrases about the deterioration of life in the Soviet Union, attempted an oddly orchestrated "coup" against the Gorbachev government, one that flopped before it ever got off the ground. Weeks later, the *Washington Post* (9/26/91) noted happily that the defeat of the coup was a triumph for the Soviet moneyed class. Among the coup's militant opponents were private entrepreneurs and thousands of members of the Russian stock exchange, who routinely made twenty times the average wage of ordinary Soviets. They headed onto "the streets of Moscow to defend their right to wheel and deal. The coup collapsed, democracy triumphed. . . . Private businessmen contributed more than 15 million rubles to buy food and equipment for the defenders." One broker was struck by how few workers responded to Yeltsin's call to defend democracy.

The boldness of this investor class in the face of an armed coup might have another explanation. A socialist critic of communism, Boris Kagarlitsky argued, "In fact, there was no coup at all." The soldiers were unarmed and confused, the tanks called out were undirected, "and the leaders of the so-called coup never even seriously tried to take power." The real coup, says Kagarlitsky, came in the aftermath when Boris Yeltsin used the incident to exceed his constitutional powers and dismantle the Soviet Union itself, absorbing all its powers into his own Russian Republic. While claiming to be undoing the "old regime," Yeltsin overthrew the new *democratic* Soviet government of 1989-1991.

In late 1993, facing strong popular resistance to his harsh free-market policies, Yeltsin went further. He forcibly disbanded the Russian parliament and every other elected representative body in the country, including municipal and regional councils. He abolished Russia's Constitutional Court and launched an armed attack upon the parliamentary building, killing an estimated two thousand resisters and demonstrators. Thousands more were jailed without charges or a trial, and hundreds of elected officials were placed under investigation.

Yeltsin banned labor unions from all political activities, suppressed dozens of publications, exercised monopoly control over all broadcast media, and permanently outlawed fifteen political parties. He unilaterally scrapped the constitution and presented the public with a new one that gave the president nearly absolute power over policy while reducing the democratically elected parliament to virtual impotence.[1] For these crimes he was hailed as a defender of democracy by U.S. leaders and media. What they most liked about Yeltsin was that he "never wavered in his support for privatization" (*San Franicsco Chronicle*, 7/6/94).[2]

Yeltsin, the "democrat," twice suspended publication of the Communist party newspaper *Pravda*. He charged it exorbitant rent for the use of its own facilities. Then in March 1992, he confiscated the paper's twelve-story building and its press and turned full ownership over to *Russiskaye Gazeta*, a government (pro-Yeltsin) newspaper.

Yeltsin's "elite" Omon troops repeatedly attacked leftist demonstrators and pickets in Moscow and other Russian cities. Parliamentary deputy Andrei Aidzerdzis, an Independent, and deputy Valentin Martemyanov, a Communist, who both vigorously opposed the Yeltsin government, were victims of political assassination. In 1994, journalist Dmitri Kholodov, who was probing corruption in high places, also was assassinated.

In 1996, Yeltsin won reelection as president, beating out a serious challenge from a communist rival. His campaign was assisted by

---

[1] The new constitution was seemingly approved in a December 1993 referendum. However, a commission appointed by Yeltsin himself found that only 46 percent of eligible voters had participated, rather than the 50 percent required to ratify a constitution (*Los Angeles Times*, 6/3/94). Little note has been taken of the fact that Yeltsin was ruling under an illegal constitution.

[2] For a more detailed account of the Yeltsin repression and the whitewash it received in the U.S. media, see "Yeltsin's Coup and the Media's Alchemy," in Michael Parenti, *Dirty Truths* (San Francisco: City Lights Books, 1996).

teams of U.S. electoral advisors, who used sophisticated polling techniques and focus groups.[3] Yeltsin also benefited from multi-million dollar donations from U.S. sources and a $10 billion aid package from the International Monetary Fund and World Bank. Equally important for victory was the crooked counting of ballots (as cursorily reported in one ABC late evening news story in July 1996).

Yeltsin exercised monopoly control over Russia's television networks, enjoying campaign coverage that amounted to nonstop promotionals. In contrast, opposition candidates were reduced to nonpersons, given only fleeting exposure, if that. Yeltsin's reelection was hailed in the West as a victory for democracy; in fact, it was a victory for private capital and monopoly media, which is not synonymous with democracy, though often treated as such by U.S. leaders and opinion makers.

Yeltsin's commitment is to captialism not democracy. In March 1996, several months before the election, when polls showed him trailing the Communist candidate, Gennadi Zyuganov, Yeltsin ordered decrees drawn up "that would have canceled the election, closed down parliament and banned the Communist Party" (*New York Times*, 7/2/96). But he was disuaded by advisors who feared the measures might incite too much resistance. Though he decided not to call off the election, "Yeltsin was never committed to turning over the government to a Communist if he lost" (*San Francisco Chronicle*, 7/26/96).

---

[3] These U.S. political consultants operated in strict secrecy lest they be seen as interfering in Russian affairs—which indeed they were. They advised Yeltsin against making extended speeches and urged more sound bites and photo opportunities. They pointed to issues and images he could exploit and ones he should avoid. Political scientist Larry Sabato, who long opposed the involvement of U.S. consultants in foreign elections, observed that Americans can be stripped of their citizenship for voting in a foreign election. "Why then should it be acceptable to influence millions of votes in a foreign election?" I would add that no foreigner is allowed to contribute money to U.S. candidates or work on their campaign staffs. But U.S. leaders can send large sums and secret teams of consultants to manipulate and sway foreign elections. Just another example of the double standard under which U.S. policy operates.

During the 1996 campaign, Yeltsin and his associates repeatedly announced that a communist victory would bring "civil war." In effect, they were voicing their willingness to discard democracy and resort to force and violence if the election did not go their way. Nor was it taken as an idle threat. At one point surveys showed that "about half the population believed that civil war would result if the Communists won" (*Sacramento Bee*, 7/9/96).

Through all of this Yeltsin received vigorous support from the White House and the U.S. media. An editorial in the *Nation* (6/17/96) asked: What if a popularly elected *communist* president in Russia had pursued Yeltsin's harsh policies of privatization, plunging his country into poverty, turning over most of its richest assets to a small segment of previous communist officials, suppressing dissident elements, using tanks to disband a popularly elected parliament that opposed his policies, re-writing the constitution to give himself almost dictatorial power, and doing all the other things Yeltsin has done? Would U.S. leaders enthusiastically devote themselves to the re-election of this "communist" president and remain all but silent about his transgressions?

The question is posed rhetorically; the *Nation* editorial presumes that the answer is no. In fact, I would respond: Yes, of course. U.S. leaders would have no trouble supporting this "communist" president, for he would be communist in name only. In actual deed he would be a devoted agent of capitalist restoration. One need only look at how successive administrations in Washington have cultivated friendly relations with the present communist leaders in China, overlooking and even explaining away their transgressions. As China's leaders open their country to private investment and growing economic inequality, they offer up a dispossessed labor force ready to work double-digit hours for subsistence pay—at enormous profit for the multinationals. U.S. politico-economic leaders know what they are doing, even if some editorial writers in this country do not. Their eye is on the money, not the color of the vessel it comes in.

Since the overthrow of communism, free-market right-wing forces in the various Eastern European countries enjoyed significant financial and organizational assistance from U.S.-financed agencies, such as the National Endowment for Democracy, the AFL-CIO's Free Trade Union Institute (a group intimately linked to the CIA), and the Free Congress Foundation, an organization with an anticommunist and conservative religious ideology.[4]

Communists and other Marxists endured political repression throughout Eastern Europe. In East Germany, the Party of Democratic Socialism had its property and offices, paid for by party members, seized in an attempt to bankrupt it. In Latvia, the communist activist Alfreds Rubics, who protested the inequities of free-market "reform," has been kept in prison for years without benefit of trial. In Lithuania, communist leaders were tortured and then imprisoned for long durations. Georgia's anticommunist president, Zviad Gamsakhurdia, incarcerated opponents from some seventy political groups without granting them a trial (*San Francisco Chronicle*, 4/17/91).

Estonia held "free elections" in which 42 percent of the population was prohibited from voting because of their Russian, Ukranian, or Belorussian antecedents. Russians and other minorities were excluded from many jobs and faced discrimination in housing and schools. Latvia also disfranchised Russians and other non-Latvian nationals, many of whom had lived in the country for almost a half century. So much for the flowering of democracy.[5]

---

[4] The reader might want to consult the late Sean Gervasi's two in-depth studies on Western destabilization of the Soviet Union: *CovertAction Quarterly*, Fall 1990 and Winter 1991-92.

[5] The focus here is mostly on the former communist countries of Eastern Europe and Russia, but similar and more bloody repressions against deposed left revolutionaries have been conducted in Afghanistan and South Yemen. In 1995, in Ethiopia, three thousand former members of Mengitsu Haile Mariam's socialist government were put on trial for executing Emperor Haile Selassie, the feudal despot who once ruled that country.

One-Way Democracy

More important than democratic rule was free-market "reform," a code word for capitalist restoration. As long as democracy could be used to destabilize one-party communist rule, it was championed by the forces of reaction. But when democracy worked *against* free-market restoration, the outcome was less tolerated.

In 1990, in Bulgaria, capitalist restoration did not go according to plan. Despite generous financial and organizational assistance from U.S. sources, including the Free Congress Foundation, the Bulgarian conservatives ended up a poor second to the communists, in what Western European observers judged to be a fair and open election. What followed was a coordinated series of strikes, demonstrations, economic pressure, acts of sabotage, and other disruptions reminiscent of CIA-orchestrated campaigns against left governments in Chile, Jamaica, Nicaragua, and British Guyana. Within five months, the free-market oppositionists forced the democratically elected communist government to resign. Bulgarian communists "complained that the U.S. had violated democratic principles in working against freely elected officials."[6]

The same pattern emerged in Albania where the democratically elected communist government won an overwhelming victory at the polls, only to face demonstrations, a general strike, economic pressure from abroad, and campaigns of disruption financed by the National Endowment for Democracy and other U.S. sources. After two months the communist government collapsed. Once the Right took power, a new law was passed denying Albanian communists and other opponents of capitalist restoration the right to vote or otherwise participate in political activities. As a reward for having extended democratic rights to all citizens, the Albanian communists and all former state employees and judges were stripped of their civil rights.

---

[6] For information on Bulgaria, see William Blum's report in *CovertAction Quarterly*, Winter 1994-95.

In the 1996 Albanian elections, the Socialists and other opposition parties—who had been predicted to do well—withdrew from the election hours before the polls closed in protest of the "blatantly rigged" vote. Election monitors from the European Union and the United States said they witnessed numerous instances of police intimidation and the stuffing of ballot boxes. The Socialist party had its final campaign rally banned and a number of prominent leaders barred from running for office because of their past communist affiliations (*New York Times*, 5/28/96). When the Socialists and their allies tried to hold protest rallies, they were attacked by Albanian security forces who beat and severely injured dozens of demonstrators (*People's Weekly World*, 5/11/96 and 6/1/96).

Openly anti-Semitic groups, cryptofascist parties, and hate campaigns surfaced in Russia, Poland, Hungary, Ukraine, Belarus, Czechoslovakia, and Rumania. Museums that commemorated the heroic antifascist resistance were closed down and monuments to the struggle against Nazism were dismantled. In countries like Lithuania, former Nazi war criminals were exonerated, some even compensated for the years they had spent in jail. Jewish cemeteries were desecrated and xenophobic attacks against foreigners of darker hue increased. With the communists no longer around, Jews and foreigners were blamed for low crop prices, inflation, crime, and other social ills.

On June 11, 1995, Lech Walesa's personal pastor, Father Henryk Jankowski, declared during a mass in Warsaw that the "Star of David is implicated in the swastika as well as in the hammer and sickle" and that the "diabolic aggressiveness of the Jews was responsible for the emergence of communism" and for World War II. The priest added that Poles should not tolerate governments made up of people who are tied to Jewish money. Walesa, who was present during the sermon, declared that his friend Jankowski was not an anti-Semite but simply "misinterpreted." Rather than retracting his comments, Jankowski spewed forth the same bile in a subsequent television interview. At about that time, placards that read "Jews to the Gas"

and "Down with the Jewish-Communist conspiracy," were visible at
a Polish Solidarity demonstration of 10,000 in Warsaw—earning not
a censorious word from church or state authorities (*Nation,* 8/7/95).

The economic policies of the fascist Pinochet regime in Chile were
openly admired by the newly installed capitalist government in
Hungary. In 1991, leading political figures and economists from the
soon-to-be abolished USSR attended a seminar on Chilean econom-
ics in Santiago and enjoyed a cordial meeting with mass murderer
General Pinochet. The Chilean dictator also was accorded a friendly
interview in *Literaturnaya Gazeta,* a major Russian publication.
Yeltsin's former security chief, Aleksandr Lebed, is a Pinochet admirer.

Instead of being transformed into capitalist states, some communist nations were entirely obliterated as political entities. Besides the
obvious example of the Soviet Union, there is the German
Democratic Republic, or East Germany, which was absorbed into the
Federal Republic of Germany. South Yemen was militarily attacked
and crushed by North Yemen. Ethiopia was occupied by Tigrean and
Eritrean forces that imprisoned large numbers of Ethiopians without
trial; expropriated Ethiopian property; suppressed Ethiopian education, business, and news media; and imposed a "systematic enforcement of tribalism in political organization and education" (Tilahun
Yilma, correspondence, *New York Times,* 4/24/96).

A systematic enforcement of tribalist political organization might
well describe Yugoslavia's fate, a nation that was fragmented by force
of arms into a number of small, conservative republics under the
suzerainty of the Western powers. With that dismemberment came a
series of wars, repressions, and atrocities committed by all contending sides.

One of Yugoslavia's first breakaway republics was Croatia, which
in 1990 was taken over by a rightist coterie, including some former
Nazi collaborators, backed by the armed might of the proto-fascist
National Guard Corps, under a constitution that relegated Serbs,
Jews, Gypsies, and Muslims to second-class status. Serbs were driven

from the civil service and police, evicted from their homes, had their businesses taken from them, and were subjected to special property taxes. Serbian newspapers in Croatia were suppressed. Many Serbs were forced from the land they had inhabited for three centuries. Still Croatia was hailed by its Western backers as a new-born democracy.

In 1996, Belarus president Alexander Lukashenko, a self-professed admirer of Adolph Hitler's organizational skills, shut down the independent newspapers and radio stations and decreed the opposition parliament defunct. Lukashenko was awarded absolute power in a referendum that claimed an inflated turnout, with no one knowing how many ballots were printed or how they were counted. Some opposition leaders fled for their lives. "Once a rich Soviet republic that produced tractors and TVs, Belarus is now [a] basket case" with a third of the population living "in deep poverty" (*San Francisco Bay Guardian,* 12/4/96).

Must We Adore Vaclav Havel?

No figure among the capitalist restorationists in the East has won more adulation from U.S. officials, media pundits, and academics than Vaclav Havel, a playwright who became the first president of post-communist Czechoslovakia and later president of the Czech Republic. The many left-leaning people who also admire Havel seem to have overlooked some things about him: his reactionary religious obscurantism, his undemocratic suppression of leftist opponents, and his profound dedication to economic inequality and an unrestrained free-market capitalism.

Raised by governesses and chauffeurs in a wealthy and fervently anticommunist family, Havel denounced democracy's "cult of objectivity and statistical average" and the idea that rational, collective social efforts should be applied to solving the environmental crisis. He called for a new breed of political leader who would rely less on "rational, cognitive thinking," show "humility in the face of the mys-

terious order of Being," and "trust in his own subjectivity as his prin-
cipal link with the subjectivity of the world." Apparently, this new
breed of leader would be a superior elitist cogitator, not unlike Plato's
philosopher king, endowed with a "sense of transcendental responsibility" and "archetypal wisdom."[7] Havel never explained how this
transcendent archetypal wisdom would translate into actual policy
decisions, and for whose benefit at whose expense.

Havel called for efforts to preserve the Christian family in the
Christian nation. Presenting himself as a man of peace and stating
that he would never sell arms to oppressive regimes, he sold weapons
to the Philippines and the fascist regime in Thailand. In June 1994,
General Pinochet, the man who butchered Chilean democracy, was
reported to be arms shopping in Czechoslovakia—with no audible
objections from Havel.

Havel joined wholeheartedly in George Bush's Gulf War, an enterprise that killed over 100,000 Iraqi civilians. In 1991, along with
other Eastern European pro-capitalist leaders, Havel voted with the
United States to condemn human rights violations in Cuba. But he
has never uttered a word of condemnation of rights violations in El
Salvador, Colombia, Indonesia, or any other U.S. client state.

In 1992, while president of Czechoslovakia, Havel, the great
democrat, demanded that parliament be suspended and he be
allowed to rule by edict, the better to ram through free-market
"reforms." That same year, he signed a law that made the advocacy of
communism a felony with a penalty of up to eight years imprisonment. He claimed the Czech constitution required him to sign it. In
fact, as he knew, the law violated the Charter of Human Rights which
is incorporated into the Czech constitution. In any case, it did not
require his signature to become law. In 1995, he supported and
signed another undemocratic law barring communists and former
communists from employment in public agencies.

---

[7] See Havel's goofy op-ed in the *New York Times* (3/1/92); it caused an embarrassed
silence among his U.S. admirers.

The propagation of anticommunism has remained a top priority for Havel. He led "a frantic international campaign" (*San Francisco Chronicle*, 2/17/95) to keep in operation two U.S.-financed, cold war radio stations, Radio Free Europe and Radio Liberty, so they could continue saturating Eastern Europe with their anticommunist propaganda.

Under Havel's government, a law was passed making it a crime to propagate national, religious, and class hatred. In effect, criticisms of big moneyed interests were now illegal, being unjustifiably lumped with ethnic and religious bigotry. Havel's government warned labor unions not to involve themselves in politics. Some militant unions had their property taken from them and handed over to compliant company unions.

In 1995, Havel announced that the "revolution" against communism would not be complete until everything was privatized. Havel's government liquidated the properties of the Socialist Union of Youth—which included camp sites, recreation halls, and cultural and scientific facilities for children—putting the properties under the management of five joint stock companies, at the expense of the youth who were left to roam the streets.

Under Czech privatization and "restitution" programs, factories, shops, estates, homes, and much of the public land was sold at bargain prices to foreign and domestic capitalists. In the Czech and Slovak republics, former aristocrats or their heirs were being given back all the lands their families had held before 1918 under the Austro-Hungarian empire, dispossessing the previous occupants and sending many of them into destitution. Havel himself took personal ownership of public properties that had belonged to his family forty years before. While presenting himself as a man dedicated to doing good for others, he did well for himself. For these reasons some of us do not have warm fuzzy feelings toward Vaclav Havel.

Colonizing the East

Once the capitalist restorationists in Eastern Europe and the former Soviet Union took state power, they worked hard to make sure that the new order of corporate plunder, individual greed, low wages, mindless pop culture, and limited electoral democracy would take hold. They set about dismantling public ownership of production and the entire network of social programs that once served the public. They integrated the erstwhile communist countries into the global capitalist system by expropriating their land, labor, natural resources, and markets, swiftly transforming them into impoverished Third World nations. All this was hailed in the U.S. corporate-owned press as a great advance for humanity.

The former communist nations are being recolonized by Western capital. Most of their foreign trade is now controlled by multinational corporations. Like Third World countries, they are increasingly deprived of each other's markets. The once heavy and mutually beneficial commerce between them has been reduced to a trickle, as their economies get tied into the investment and extractive needs of global capitalism. Instead of mutual development, they are now experiencing the maldevelopment imposed by global monopoly capital.

Multinational corporations are moving into Russia to exploit vast oil and natural gas reserves and rich mineral deposits at great profit to themselves and with little benefit to the Russian people. Over the protests of U.S. and Russian environmentalists, U.S. timber interests, with financial support from a venture fund sponsored by the Pentagon, are preparing to clear-cut the Siberian wilderness, a region that holds one-fifth of the planet's forests and is the habitat of many rare species (*New York Times*, 1/30/96).

All aid to the former communist countries is funneled into the private sector. As noted in the *Guardian* (11/19/94), "The hundreds of millions of dollars spawned by Western aid programs have mainly benefited the Western companies which headed east to board the aid gravy train." When Rumania inaugurated an over-the-counter market for trading privatization shares, the $20 million in "start-up costs were largely covered by the U.S. Agency for International Development" (*Wall St. Journal*, 9/17/96).

In 1996, the International Monetary Fund extended a $10.2 billion loan to Russia, with terms calling for the privatization of agriculture and other state-owned assets, and the elimination of human service and fuel subsidies. U.S. aid is used to help private investors buy public properties and extract publicly owned raw materials from Eastern European countries under the most favorable investment conditions.

With the advent of private investment in the East, production did not grow as promised but dropped drastically. Hundreds of the more attractive and solvent state enterprises have been privatized, often given away at token prices to foreign investors, while other state firms are decapitalized or driven into bankruptcy. Between 1989 and 1995, in what is now the Czech Republic, nearly 80 percent of all enterprises were privatized—and industrial production shrank by two-thirds. Privatization in Poland caused production to shrink one-third between 1989 and 1992. Vast electronic and high-tech complexes in East Germany, employing tens of thousands of workers, have been taken over by giant West German firms and then closed down. Under privatization, much of the former Soviet Union's scientific and technical infrastructure is disintegrating, along with its physical plants.

Since going private, ZiL, the huge Moscow plant, saw its production of trucks slump from 150,000 to 13,000 a year, with almost 40 percent of the workforce laid off. In April 1996, the remaining workers petitioned the Russian government to take back control of ZiL. In the past, ZiL workers and their relatives "had unshakeably safe jobs" at the factory. They lived in apartments and attended schools provided by ZiL. As babies they spent their days at the ZiL day care center, and when ill they were attended to by ZiL doctors. "I was raised in a country that cared about its workers," said one machinist, who now was sorry he had opposed that system (*New York Times*, 5/8/94).

In Macedonia, one of the breakaway republics of Yugoslavia, a labor representative noted, "Privatization seems to mean the destruction of our companies." Macedonians seemed more troubled by free-market economic hardships than by the much publicized ethnic rivalries. They complained about how work has taken over their lives: "One has no time to care about others; there's no time even for oneself—only time for making money" (PBS-TV report, 1/16/95).

Agricultural output of grain, corn, livestock, and other products plummeted in the former communist countries, as thousands of cooperative farms were forcibly broken up. The new private farmers have small plots, often cannot get loans, seeds, fertilizer, or machinery, and are rapidly losing their holdings or reverting to subsistence farming. Hungary's agricultural cooperatives had been one sector of the socialist economy that performed well. But with privatization, farm output tumbled 40 percent in 1993 (*Los Angeles Times*, 1/29/94).

A drastic deterioration in agricultural production occurred in Bulgaria, once considered the breadbasket of Eastern Europe, causing severe bread shortages by 1996. Bulgaria was also suffering from a 20 percent monthly inflation and was sinking into that familiar cycle of foreign debt: cutting back on services to qualify for IMF loans, borrowing to pay off past borrowing. "The [Bulgarian] government must impose more free market austerity measures to get vital international loans to repay portions of the $9.4 billion foreign debt" (*San Francisco Chronicle*, 7/18/96).

In 1992, the Lithuanian government decreed that former owners and their descendants could reclaim property confiscated during the socialist era. As a result, tens of thousands of farming families, about 70 percent of the rural population, were evicted from land they had worked for over a half century, destroying the country's agricultural base in the process.

Much production in East Germany was dismantled to prevent competition with West German firms. This was especially evident when collective agriculture was broken up to protect the heavily subsidized and less productive private farms of West Germany.[8] Without making compensation, West German capitalists grabbed almost all the socialized property in the GDR, including factories, mills, farms, apartments and other real estate, and the medical care system— assets worth about $2 trillion—in what has amounted to the largest expropriation of public wealth by private capital in European history.

The end result of all this free-market privatization in East Germany is that rents, once 5 percent of one's income, have climbed to as much as two-thirds; likewise the costs of transportation, child care, health care, and higher education have soared beyond the reach of many.

East Germans of various political stripes have a number of complaints: (a) The net money flow has been East to West, in what amounts to a colonization of the East. (b) The free market is a myth; the West German economy is heavily subsidized and fully regulated but against the interests of the East. (c) West German police are much more brutal than were the East German police. (d) If West Germany had denazified anywhere near as thoroughly as it forced the East to desocialize, it would be a totally different country (*Z Magazine*, 7/92).

On that last point it should be noted that German officials are bringing criminal charges against those who "collaborated" with the GDR of East Germany in any official capacity, including even teachers and minor administrators.[9]

Emigrés from Communist states are astonished by the amount of bureaucracy they find in the West. Two Soviet immigrants to Canada complained, independently of each other, that "bureaucracy here

---

[8] See Robert McIntyre's report in *Monthly Review,* 12/93.
[9] Several thousand former GDR officials, judges, and others have been imprisoned or are facing prison terms for "treason." See the discussion in chapter five.

was even worse than at home" (*Monthly Review,* 5/88). East Germans living in the West were staggered by the flood of complicated forms they had to fill out for taxes, health insurance, life insurance, unemployment compensation, job retraining, rent subsidies, and bank accounts. Furthermore, "because of the kind of personal information they had to give, they felt more observed and spied on than they were by the Stasi [the GDR security police]" (*Z Magazine,* 7/92).

Soviet Jews who emigrated to Israel during the cold war era experienced a similar disillusionment with the difficulties of life and lack of idealism. The discouraging letters they sent home were considered an important factor in the drop in immigration from the USSR to Israel.

With the capitalist restoration in full swing, the peoples of the former communist nations had ample opportunity to learn what life was like in the free-market paradise. Their experiences are detailed in the next chapter.

CHAPTER 7

THE FREE-MARKET PARADISE
GOES EAST (II)

Free-market propagandists in the former communist countries claimed that, as capital was privatized and accumulated in a few hands, production would be stimulated and prosperity would be at hand. But first, there would be a "difficult period" to go through. The difficult period is proving to be far more severe and protracted than predicted, and may well be the permanent condition of capitalist restoration.

For Vipers and Bloodsuckers

In 1990, as the Soviet Union was preparing for its fatal plunge into the free-market paradise, Bruce Gelb, head of the United States Information Agency, told a reporter that the Soviets would benefit economically from U.S. business education because "the vipers, the bloodsuckers, the middlemen — that's what needs to be rehabilitated in the Soviet Union. That's what makes our kind of country click!" (*Washington Post*, 6/11/90)

Today, the former communist countries and China are clicking away with vipers and bloodsuckers. Thousands of luxury cars have appeared on the streets of Moscow and Prague. Rents and real estate prices have skyrocketed. Numerous stock exchanges have sprung up in China and Eastern Europe, sixteen in the former USSR alone. And a new class of investors, speculators, and racketeers are wallowing in wealth. The professed goal is no longer to provide a better life for all citizens but to maximize the opportunities for individuals to accumulate personal fortunes.

More opulence for the few creates more poverty for the many. As one young female journalist in Russia put it: "Everytime someone gets richer, I get poorer" (*New York Times*, 10/15/95). In Russia, the living standard of the average family has fallen almost by half since the market "reforms" took hold (*New York Times*, 6/16/96). A report from Hungary makes the same point: "While the 'new rich' live in villas with a Mercedes parked in a garage, the number of poor people has been growing" (*New York Times*, 2/27/90).

As socialist Vietnam opens itself to foreign investment and the free market, "gaps between rich and poor . . . have widened rapidly" and "the quality of education and health care for the poor has deteriorated" (*New York Times*, 4/8/96). Prosperity has come "only to a privileged few in Vietnam" leading to "an emerging class structure that is at odds with the country's professed egalitarian ideals" (AP report, 10/28/96).

In the emerging free-market paradise of Russia and Eastern Europe, price deregulation produced not competitive prices but prices set by private monopolies, adding to the galloping inflation. Beggars, pimps, dope pushers, and other hustlers ply their trades as never before. And there has been a dramatic rise in unemployment, homelessness, air and water pollution, prostitution, spousal abuse, child abuse, and just about every other social ill.[1]

---

[1] Vladimir Bilenkin, "Russian Workers Under the Yeltsin Regime: Notes on a Class in Defeat," *Monthly Review*, 11/96, 1-12.

In countries like Russia and Hungary, as widely reported in the U.S. press, the suicide rate has climbed by 50 percent in a few years. Reductions in fuel service, brought about by rising prices and unpaid bills, have led to a growing number of deaths or serious illnesses among the poor and the elderly during the long winters.

In Russia, doctors and nurses in public clinics are now grossly underpaid. Free health clinics are closing. More than ever, hospitals suffer from unsanitary conditions and shortages of disposable syringes, needles, vaccines, and modern equipment. Many hospitals now have no hot water, some no water at all.[2] The deterioration of immunization programs and health standards has allowed polio to make a serious comeback, along with tuberculosis, cholera, diptheria, dysentery, and sexually transmitted diseases. Drug addiction has risen sharply. "Russia's hospitals are struggling to treat increasing numbers of addicts with decreasing levels of funding" (CNN news report, 2/2/92).

There has been a decline in nutritional levels and a sharp increase in stress and illness. Yet the number of visits to doctors has dropped by half because fees are so costly in the newly privatized health care systems. As a result, many illnesses go undetected and untreated until they become critical. Russian military officials describe the health of conscripts as "catastrophic." Within the armed forces suicides have risen dramatically and deaths from drug overdoses have climbed 80 percent in recent years. (*Toronto Star*, 11/5/95).

The overthrow of communism brought a rising infant mortality and soaring death rates in Russia, Bulgaria, Hungary, Latvia, Moldavia, Rumania, Ukraine, Mongolia, and East Germany. One-third of Russian men never live to sixty years of age. In 1992, Russia's birth rate fell below its death rate for the first time since World War II. In 1992 and 1993, East Germans buried two people for every baby

---

[2] See Eleanor Randolph, *Waking the Tempests: Ordinary Life in the New Russia* (New York: Simon & Schuster, 1996).

born. The death rate rose nearly 20 percent for East German women in their late thirties, and nearly 30 percent for men of the same age (*New York Times*, 4/6/94).

With the end of subsidized rents, estimates of homelessness in Moscow alone run as high as 300,000. The loss of resident permits deprives the homeless of medical care and other state benefits, such as they are. Dressed in rags and victimized by both mobsters and government militia, thousands of indigents die of cold and hunger on the streets of various cities. In Rumania, thousands of homeless children live in sewers and train stations, sniffing glue to numb their hunger, begging and falling prey to various predators (National Public Radio news, 7/21/96).

In Mongolia, hundreds of homeless children live in the sewers of Ulaanbaatar. Before 1990, Mongolia was a prosperous nation that had benefited from Soviet and East European financial assistance and technical aid. Its new industrial centers produced leather goods, woolen products, textiles, cement, meat, grain, and timber. "The communist era dramatically improved the quality of life of the people . . . achieving commendable levels of social development through state-sponsored social welfare measures," but free-market privatization and deindustrialization has brought unemployment, mass poverty, and widespread malnutrition to Mongolia.[3]

Shock Therapy for the Many

Unemployment rates have risen as high as 30 percent in countries that once knew full employment under communism. One Polish worker claims that the jobless are pretty much unemployable after age 40. Polish women say economic demise comes earlier for them, since to get a job, as one puts it, "you must be young, childless and

---

[3] K.L. Abeywickrama, "The Marketization of Mongolia," *Monthly Review*, 3/96, 25-33, and reports cited therein.

have a big bosom" (*Nation*, 12/7/92). Occupational safety is now almost nonexistent and workplace injuries and deaths have drastically increased.

Workers now toil harder and longer for less, often in sweatshop conditions. Teachers, scientists, factory workers, and countless others struggle for months without pay as their employers run out of funds (*Los Angeles Times*, 1/17/96). The waves of strikes and work stoppages in Russia and Eastern Europe are accorded unsympathetic press treatment in those countries.

Even in the few remaining countries in which communist governments retain control, such as China, Vietnam, and Cuba, the opening to private investment has contributed to a growing inequality. In Cuba, the dollar economy has brought with it a growth in prostitution (including girls as young as eleven and twelve), street beggers, and black-market dealings with tourists (Avi Chomsky, *Cuba Update*, 9/96).

In China, there are workers who now put in twelve- to sixteen-hour days for subsistence pay, without regularly getting a day off. Those who protest against poor safety and health conditions risk being fired or jailed. The market reforms in China have also brought a return of child labor (*San Francisco Chronicle*, 8/14/90). "I think this is what happens when you have private companies," says Ms. Peng, a young migrant who has doubts about the new China. "In private companies, you know, the workers don't have rights" (*Wall St. Journal*, 5/19/94).

Throughout Eastern Europe, unions have been greatly weakened or broken. Sick leave, maternity leave, paid vacations, and other job benefits once taken for granted under communism have been cut or abolished. Worker sanitariums, vacation resorts, health clinics, sports and cultural centers, children's nurseries, day-care centers, and other features that made communist enterprises more than just workplaces, have nearly vanished. Rest homes formerly reserved for workers have been privatized and turned into casinos, night clubs, and restaurants for the nouveau riche.[4]

Real income has shrunk by as much as 30 to 40 percent in the ex-communist countries. In 1992 alone, Russia saw its consumer spending drop by 38 percent. (By comparison, during the Great Depression, consumer spending in the United States fell 21 percent over four years.) In both Poland and Bulgaria, an estimated 70 percent now live below or just above the poverty line. In Russia, it is 75 to 85 percent, with a third of the population barely subsisting in absolute economic desperation. In Hungary, which has received most of the West's investment in Eastern Europe, over one-third of its citizens live in abject poverty, and 70 percent of the men hold two or more jobs, working up to 14 hours a day, according to the Ministry of Labor.

After months of not getting paid, coal miners in far eastern Russia were beginning to starve. By August 1996, 10,000 of them had stopped working simply because they were too weak from hunger. With no coal being extracted, the region's power plants began to shut down, threatening an electrical blackout that would further harm the nation's Pacific coastal industry and trade (*Los Angeles Times,* 8/3/96).

Eastern Europeans are witnessing scenes "that are commonplace enough in the West, but are still wrenching here: the old man rummaging through trash barrels for castaway items, the old woman picking through a box of bones at a meat market in search of one with enough gristle to make a thin soup" (*Los Angeles Times,* 3/10/90). With their savings and pensions swallowed up by inflation, elderly pensioners crowd the sidewalks of Moscow selling articles of their

---

[4] One booming employment area is the business security forces and private armies, which in the Soviet Union alone muster some 800,000 men. "Another employer of choice for working class youth is the immense state apparatus of repression which is now more formidable than that of the Soviet period. Today, this apparatus is numerically superior to the Armed Forces, better paid and better equipped. The regime's real enemy is inside, after all": Bilenkin, "Russian Workers Under the Yeltsin Regime," *Monthly Review,* 11/96, 7.

clothing and other pathetic wares, while enduring harassment by police and thugs (*Washington Post*, 1/1/96). A Russian senior citizen refers to "this poverty, which only a few have escaped" while some "have become wildly rich." (*Modern Maturity*, September/October 1994).

Crime and Corruption

With the socialist ethic giving way to private greed, corruption assumed virulent new forms in the post-Communist nations. Officials high and low are on the take, including the police. The Russian security minister calculated that one-third of Russian oil and one-half of Russian nickel shipped out of the country was stolen. Among those enjoying "staggering profits" from this plunder were Shell Oil and British Petroleum (*Washington Post*, 2/2/93). In April 1992, the chairman of Russia's central bank admitted that at least $20 billion had been illegally taken out of the country and deposited in Western banks (*Nation*, 4/19/93).

Choice chunks of public real estate are quietly sold off at a fraction of their value in exchange for payoffs to the officials who preside over the sales. Government officials buy goods from private contractors at twice the normal price in exchange for kickbacks. Factory directors sell state-made commodities at low state prices to their own private firms, which those firms then resell at market prices for a vast profit. One member of the Moscow City Council estimated that corruption amounted to hundreds of billions of dollars. If these funds went into state coffers instead of private pockets "we could meet our budget three or four times over" (*Los Angeles Times*, 7/10/92).

Along with corruption, there is an upsurge in organized crime. Over one hundred racket syndicates in Russia now extort tribute from 80 percent of all enterprises. From 1992 to 1995, as competition for the spoils of "reform" intensified, forty-six of Russia's more prominent businessmen were slain in gangland-style murders. In

1994, there were more than 2500 contract murders, almost all of them unsolved. "Contract murders occur regularly now in Russia, and most go without much notice" (*San Francisco Chronicle,* 11/17/95). Police say they lack the funds, personnel, and crime detection equipment for any real campaign against the mobs.

Street crime also has increased sharply (*New York Times,* 5/7/96). In the former Soviet Union, women and elderly who once felt free to sit in parks late at night now dare not venture out after dark. Since the overthrow of communism in Hungary, thefts and other felonies have nearly tripled and there has been a 50 percent increase in homicides (NPR, 2/24/92). The police force in Prague today is many times greater than it was under communism, when "relatively few police were needed" (*New York Times,* 12/18/91). How odd that fewer police were needed in the communist police state than in the free-market paradise.

In the Republic of Georgia, life has been reduced to a level of violent chaos never imagined under communism. Criminal rings control much of the commerce, and paramilitary groups control most of the criminal rings. No longer able to sell its goods on the Soviet market but unable to compete on the international market, Georgian industry has experienced a massive decline and, as in most Eastern countries, the public debt has leaped upward while real wages have shrunk painfully (*San Francisco Chronicle,* 7/20/93).

Cultural Decay

Cultural life has drastically declined in the former communist countries. Theaters are sparsely attended because tickets are now prohibitively expensive. Publicly owned movie industries in countries like Russia, Poland, Czechoslovakia, and the German Democratic Republic, which produced a number of worthwhile films, have been defunded or bought out by Western business interests and now make cartoons, commercials, and music videos. Movie houses have been taken over by corporate chains and offer many of the same Hollywood junk films that we have the freedom to see.

Subsidies for the arts and literature have been severely cut. Symphony orchestras have disbanded or taken to playing at block parties and other minor occasions. The communist countries used to produce inexpensive but quality editions of classical and contemporary authors and poets, including ones from Latin America, Asia, and Africa. These have been replaced by second-rate, mass-market publications from the West. During the communist era, three of every five books in the world were produced in the Soviet Union. Today, as the cost of books, periodicals, and newspapers has skyrocketed and education has declined, readership has shrunk almost to Third World levels.

Books of a Marxist or otherwise critical left perspective have been removed from bookstores and libraries. In East Germany, the writers' association reported one instance in which 50,000 tons of books, some brand new, were buried in a dump. The German authorities who disposed of the books apparently did not feel quite free enough to burn them.

Education, once free, is now accessible only to those who can afford the costly tuition rates. The curricula have been "depoliticized," meaning that a left perspective critical of imperialism and capitalism has been replaced by a conservative one that is supportive or at least uncritical of these forces.

Descending upon the unhappy societies of Eastern Europe and Russia are the Hare Krishnas, Mormans, Moonies, Jehovah's Witnesses, Bahais, rightist Christian evangelicals, self-improvement hucksters, instant-success peddlers, and other materialistic spiritualist scavengers who prey upon the deprived and the desperate, offering solace in the next world or the promise of wealth and success in this one.

The president of one of Russia's largest construction companies summed it up: "All the material well-being that people had, they lost in one hour. There is practically no more free medical care, accessible higher education, no right to a job or rest. The houses of culture, libraries, stadiums, kindergartens and nurseries, pioneer camps, schools, hospitals and stores are closing. The cost of housing, communal services and transport are no longer affordable for the majority of families" (*People's Weekly World*, 4/6/96).

Facing forced privatization, news and entertainment media have had to find rich owners, corporate advertisers, conservative foundations, or agencies within the newly installed capitalist governments to finance them. Television and radio programs that had a left perspective, including some popular youth shows, have been removed from the air. All media have been purged of leftists and restaffed by people with acceptable ideological orientations. This process of moving toward a procapitalist communication monopoly has been described in the Western media as "democratization." Billboards and television commercials promoting U.S. cigarettes, automobiles, and other consumer items — many of them beyond the average pocketbook — now can be seen everywhere.

Women and Children Last

The overthrow of communism has brought a sharp increase in gender inequality. The new constitution adopted in Russia eliminates provisions that guaranteed women the right to paid maternity leave, job security during pregnancy, prenatal care, and affordable day-care centers.[5] Without the former communist stipulation that women get at least one third of the seats in any legislature, female political representation has dropped to as low as 5 percent in some countries.

In all communist countries about 90 percent of women had jobs in what was a full-employment economy. Today, women compose

---

[5] Under Soviet law, women had been granted four months off with full pay for childbirth, and a year of partial pay if they elected to stay home with the child. In addition, they were allowed up to three years leave with a guarantee that their jobs would be held for them.

over two-thirds of the unemployed. Those who do work are being channeled into low-pay unskilled positions. Women are being driven from the professions in disproportionate numbers and are advised against getting professional training. More than 30 percent of unemployed females are skilled workers and professionals who previously earned higher salaries than the national norm. The loss of maternity benefits and child care services has created still greater obstacles to female employment.

Throughout the Eastern European nations, the legal, financial, and psychological independence that women enjoyed under socialism has been undermined. Divorce, abortion, and birth control are more difficult to obtain. Released from the "Soviet yoke," the autonomous region of Ingushetia decriminalized polygamy and made it legal for women to be sold into marriage. Instances of sexual harassment and violence against women have increased sharply. In Russia, the number of women murdered annually—primarily by husbands and boyfriends—skyrocketed from 5,300 to 15,000 in the first three years of the free-market paradise. In 1994, an additional 57,000 women were seriously injured in such assaults. These official figures understate the level of violence. The Communist party committees that used to intervene in cases of domestic abuse no longer exist.

Women also are being recruited in unprecedented numbers for the booming sex industry that caters to foreign and domestic businessmen. Unable to find employment in the professions for which they originally were trained, many highly educated Russian and Eastern European women go abroad to work as prostitutes. Women are not the only ones being channeled into the sex market. As reported in *Newsweek* (9/2/96):

> Prague and Budapest now rival Bangkok and Manila as hubs for the collection of children to serve visiting pedophiles. Last year one investigator was stunned to find stacks of child pornography in the reception rooms of Estonia'a Parliament and its social welfare department. "Free love is regarded as one of the new 'freedoms' which the

market economy can offer," she wrote. "Simultaneously, sex in the market economy has also become a profitable commodity." In some cases "children are kidnapped and held like slaves," says [Thomas] Kattau [a specialist with the Council of Europe]. "This is happening more and more. It is organized crime."

Life conditions for children have deteriorated greatly throughout the ex-communist world. Free summer camps have been closed down. School lunches, once free or low-priced, are now too costly for many pupils. Hungry children constitute a serious school problem. Instead of attending classes, chidren can be found hawking drinks or begging in the streets. Juvenile crime is booming along with juvenile prostitution, while funds for youth rehabilitation services dwindle (*Los Angeles Times*, 7/15/94).

"We Didn't Realize What We Had"

While many Eastern European intellectuals remain fervent champions of the free-market paradise, most workers and peasants no longer romanticize capitalism, having felt its unforgiving lash. "We didn't realize what we had" has become a common refrain. "The latest public opinion surveys show that many Russians consider Brezhnev's era and even Stalin's era to have been better than the present-day period, at least as far as economic conditions and personal safety are concerned" (*New York Times*, 10/15/95). A joke circulating in Russia in 1992 went like this: Q. What did capitalism accomplish in one year that communism could not do in seventy years? A. Make communism look good.

Throughout Eastern Europe and the former USSR, many people grudgingly admitted that conditions were better under communism (*New York Times*, 3/30/95). Pro-capitalist Angela Stent, of Georgetown University, allows that "most people are worse off than they were under Communism . . . . The quality of life has deteriorated with the spread of crime and the disappearance of the social safety net" (*New York Times*, 12/20/93). An East German steelworker is quoted as saying "I do not know if there is a future for me, and I'm not too hopeful. The fact is, I lived better under Communism" (*New York Times*, 3/3/91). An elderly Polish woman, reduced to one Red Cross meal a day: "I'm not Red but I have to say life for poor people was better before. . . . Now things are good for businessmen but not for us poor" (*New York Times*, 3/17/91). One East German woman commented that the West German women's movement was only beginning to fight for "what we already had here. . . . We took it for granted because of the socialist system. Now we realize what we [lost]" (*Los Angeles Times*, 8/6/91).

Anticommunist dissidents who labored hard to overthrow the GDR were soon voicing their disappointments about German reunification. One noted Lutheran clergyman commented: "We fell into the tyranny of money. The way wealth is distributed in this society [capitalist Germany] is something I find very hard to take." Another Lutheran pastor said: "We East Germans had no real picture of what life was like in the West. We had no idea how competitive it would be. . . . Unabashed greed and economic power are the levers that move this society. The spiritual values that are essential to human happiness are being lost or made to seem trivial. Everything is buy, earn, sell" (*New York Times*, 5/26/96).

Maureen Orth asked the first woman she met in a market if her life had changed in the last two years and the woman burst into tears. She was 58 years old, had worked forty years in a potato factory and now could not afford most of the foods in the market: "It's not life, it's just existence," she said (*Vanity Fair*, 9/94). Orth interviewed the chief of a hospital department in Moscow who said: "Life was different two years ago—I was a human being." Now he had to chauffeur people around for extra income. What about the new freedoms? "Freedom for what?" he responded. "Freedom to buy a pornographic magazine?"

In a similar vein, former GDR defense minister Heinz Kessler commented: "Sure, I hear about the new freedom that people are enjoying in Eastern Europe. But how do you define freedom? Millions of people in Eastern Europe are now free from employment, free from safe streets, free from health care, free from social security" (*New York Times,* 7/20/96).

Do people in the East want the free market? Opinion polls taken in late 1993 in Russia showed only 27 percent of all respondents supported a market economy. By large majorities, people believed that state control over prices and over private business is "useful," and that "the state should provide everyone with a job and never tolerate unemployment." In Poland, 92 percent wanted to keep the state welfare system, and lopsided majorities wanted to retain subsidized housing and foods and return to full employment (*Monthly Review,* 12/94). "Most people here," reports a *New York Times* Moscow correspondent (6/23/96), "are suspicious of private property, wonder what was so bad about a system that supplied health care at low cost from birth to death, and hope that prices are once again reined in by the government."

One report from Russia describes "a bitter electorate, which has found life under a democrat [meaning Yeltsin!] worse than under the now-departed Communists" (*New York Times,* 12/18/91). A report from Warsaw refers to the "free-market economic transformation that most Poles no longer support" (*Washington Post,* 12/15/91). People's biggest fears are inflation, unemployment, crime, and pollution.

State socialism, "the system that did not work," provided everyone with some measure of security. Free-market capitalism, "the system that works," brought a free-falling economy, financial plunder, deteriorating social conditions, and mass suffering.

In reaction, Eastern European voters have been returning Communists to office—to preside over the ruin and wreckage of broken nations. By 1996, former Communists and their allies had won significant victories in Russia, Bulgaria, Poland, Hungary, Lithuania, and Estonia, sometimes emerging as the strongest blocs in their respective parliaments. This was achieved in the face of the same intimidations, police harassments, monetary disadvantages, restrictive ballot access, media shutout, and fraudulent vote counts that confront leftist parties in most "democratic capitalist" countries.

When the first anticommunist upheavals began in Eastern Europe in 1989, there were those on the Left who said that if the people in those countries discovered that they didn't like the free-market system they could always return to some variant of socialism. As I argued at the time, this was hardly a realistic view. Capitalism is not just an economic system but an entire social order. Once it takes hold, it is not voted out of existence by electing socialists or communists. They may occupy office but the wealth of the nation, the basic property relations, organic law, financial system, and debt structure, along with the national media, police power, and state institutions, have all been fundamentally restructured. The resources needed for social programs and full employment have been pilfered or completely obliterated, as have monetary reserves, markets, and natural resources. A few years of untrammeled free-market marauding has left these nations at the point of no foreseeable return.

The belief propagated by the free-market "reformers" is that the transition from socialism to capitalism can only be made through a vast private accumulation of capital. The hardship inflicted by such privatization supposedly is only temporary. The truth is, nations get stuck in that "temporary" stage for centuries. One need only look at Latin America.

Like other Third World nations, the former communist countries are likely to remain in poverty indefinitely, so that a privileged few may continue to enjoy greater and greater opulence at the expense of the many. To secure that arrangement, the corporate class will resort to every known manipulation and repression against democratic resurgence. In these endeavors they will have the expert assistance of international capital, the CIA, and other agencies of state capitalist domination.

According to Noam Chomsky, communism "was a monstrosity," and "the collapse of tyranny" in Eastern Europe and Russia is "an occasion for rejoicing for anyone who values freedom and human dignity."[6] I treasure freedom and human dignity yet find no occasion for rejoicing. The postcommunist societies do not represent a net gain for such values. If anything, the breakup of the communist states has brought a colossal victory for global capitalism and imperialism, with its correlative increase in human misery, and a historic setback for revolutionary liberation struggles everywhere. There will be harder times ahead even for modestly reformist nationalist governments, as the fate of Panama and Iraq have indicated. The breakup also means a net loss of global pluralism and a more intensive socio-economic inequality throughout the world.[7]

The peoples of Eastern Europe believed they were going to keep all the social gains they had enjoyed under communism while adding on all the consumerism of the West. Many of their grievances about existing socialism were justified but their romanticized image of the capitalist West was not. They had to learn the hard way. Expecting to advance from Second World to First World status, they have been rammed down into the Third World, ending up like capitalist Indonesia, Mexico, Zaire, and Turkey. They wanted it all and have been left with almost nothing.

---

[6] Noam Chomsky, *Powers and Prospects* (Boston: South End Press, 1996), 83.
[7] The overthrow of communism, however, does not mean the end of the U.S. global military machine. Quite the contrary, huge sums continue to be spent, and new weapons systems and high-tech methods of killing continue to be developed in order that a tight grip be kept on the world by those who own it.

CHAPTER 8

THE END OF MARXISM?

Some people say Marxism is a science and others say it is a dogma, a bundle of reductionist unscientific claims. I would suggest that Marxism is not a science in the positivist sense, formulating hypotheses and testing for predictability, but more accurately a social science, one that shows us how to conceptualize systematically and systemically, moving from surface appearances to deeper, broader features, so better to understand both the specific and the general, and the relationship between the two.

Marxism has an explanatory power that is superior to mainstream bourgeois social science because it deals with the imperatives of class power and political economy, the motor forces of society and history. The class basis of political economy is not a subject for which mainstream social science has much understanding or tolerance.[1] In 1915, Lenin wrote that "[bourgeois] science will not even hear of Marxism, declaring that it has been refuted and annihilated. Marx is attacked

---

[1] This aversion to recognizing the realities of class power exists even among many who consider themselves to be on the Left; see the discussion on the Anything-But-Class theorists in the next chapter.

with equal zest by young scholars who are making a career by refuting socialism, and by decrepit elders who are preserving the tradition of all kinds of outworn systems."

Over eighty years later, the careerist scholars are still declaring Marxism to have been proven wrong once and for all. As the anticommunist liberal writer, Irving Howe, put it: "The simplistic formulae of textbooks, including the Marxist ones, no longer hold. That is why some of us . . . don't regard ourselves as Marxists" (*Newsday*, 4/21/86). Here I want to argue that Marxism is not outmoded or simplistic, only the image of it entertained by anti-Marxists like Howe.

Some Durable Basics

With the overthrow of communist governments in Eastern Europe and the Soviet Union, announcements about the moribund nature of "Marxist dogma" poured forth with renewed vigor. But Marx's major work was *Capital*, a study not of "existing socialism," which actually did not exist in his day, but of capitalism—a subject that remains terribly relevant to our lives. It would make more sense to declare Marxism obsolete if and when *capitalism* is abolished, rather than socialism. I wish to argue not merely that Marx is still relevant but that he is more relevant today than he was in the nineteenth century, that the forces of capitalist motion and development are operating with greater scope than when he first studied them.

This is not to say that everything Marx and Engels anticipated has come true. Their work was not a perfect prophecy but an imperfect, incomplete science (like all sciences), directed toward understanding a capitalism that leaves its bloody footprints upon the world as never before. Some of Marxism's basic postulates are as follows:

In order to live, human beings must produce. People cannot live by bread alone but neither can they live without bread. This does not mean all human activity can be reduced to material motives but that all activity is linked to a material base. A work of art may have no direct economic motive attached to it, yet its creation would be impossible if there did not exist the material conditions that allowed the artist to create and show the work to interested audiences who have the time for art.

What people need for survival is found in nature but rarely in a form suitable for immediate consumption. Labor therefore becomes a primary condition of human existence. But labor is more than a way of providing for survival. It is one of the means whereby people develop their material and cultural life, acquiring knowledge, and new modes of social organization. The conflicting class interests that evolve around the productive forces shape the development of a social system. When we speak of early horticultural societies, or of slave or feudal or mercantile or industrial capitalist societies, we are recognizing how the basic economic relations leave a defining stamp on a given social order.

Capitalist theorists present capital as a creative providential force. As they would have it, capital gives shape and opportunity to labor; capital creates production, jobs, new technologies, and a general prosperity. Marxists turn the equation around. They argue that, of itself, capital cannot produce anything; it is the thing that is produced by labor. Only human labor can create the farm and the factory, the machine and the computer. And in a class society, the wealth so produced by many is accumulated in the hands of relatively few who soon translate their economic power into political and cultural power in order to better secure the exploitative social order that so favors them.

The standard "trickle down" theory says that the accumulation of wealth at the top eventually brings more prosperity to the rest of us below; a rising tide lifts all boats. I would argue that in a class society the accumulation of wealth fosters the spread of poverty. The wealthy few live off the backs of the impoverished many. There can be no rich slaveholders living in idle comfort without a mass of penniless slaves to support their luxurious life style, no lords of the manor who live in opulence without a mass of impoverished landless serfs who till the lords' lands from dawn to dusk. So too under capitalism, there can be no financial moguls and industrial tycoons without millions of underpaid and overworked employees.

Exploitation can be measured not only in paltry wages, but in the disparity between the wealth created by the worker and the pay she or he receives. Thus some professional athletes receive dramatically higher salaries than most people, but compared to the enormous wealth they produce for their owners, and taking into account the rigors and relative brevity of their careers, the injuries sustained, and the lack of life-long benefits, it can be said they are exploited at a far higher rate than most workers.

Conservative ideologues defend capitalism as the system that preserves culture, traditional values, the family, and community. Marxists would respond that capitalism has done more to undermine such things than any other system in history, given its wars, colonizations, and forced migrations, its enclosures, evictions, poverty wages, child labor, homelessness, underemployment, crime, drug infestation, and urban squalor.

All over the world, community in the broader sense—the Gemeinschaft with its organic social relationships and strong reciprocal bonds of commonality and kinship—is forcibly transformed by global capital into commercialized, atomized, mass-market societies. In the *Communist Manifesto*, Marx and Engels referred to capitalism's implacable drive to settle "over the whole surface of the globe," creating "a world after its own image." No system in history has been more relentless in battering down ancient and fragile cultures, pulverizing centuries-old practices in a matter of years, devouring the resources of whole regions, and standardizing the varieties of human experience.

Big Capital has no commitment to anything but capital accumulation, no loyalty to any nation, culture, or people. It moves inexorably according to its inner imperative to accumulate at the highest possible rate without concern for human and environmental costs. The first law of the market is to make the largest possible profit from other people's labor. Private profitability rather than human need is the determining condition of private investment. There prevails a rational systematization of human endeavor in pursuit of a *socially* irrational end: "accumulate, accumulate, accumulate."

More Right than Wrong

Those who reject Marx frequently contend that his predictions about proletariat revolution have proven wrong. From this, they conclude that his analysis of the nature of capitalism and imperialism must also be wrong. But we should distinguish between Marx the chiliastic thinker, who made grandly optimistic predictions about the flowering of the human condition, and Marx the economist and social scientist, who provided us with fundamental insights into capitalist society that have held painfully true to the present day. The latter Marx has been regularly misrepresented by anti-Marxist writers. Consider the following predictions:

Business Cycles and the Tendency toward Recession. Marx noted that something more than greed is involved in the capitalist's relentless pursuit of profit. Given the pressures of competition and rising wages, capitalists must make technological innovations to increase their productivity and diminish their labor costs. This creates problems of its own. The more capital goods (such as machinery, plants, technologies, fuels) needed for production, the higher the fixed costs and the greater the pressure to increase productivity to maintain profit margins.[2]

---

[2] As an industry becomes more capital intensive, proportionately more money must be invested to generate a given number of jobs. But business is not dedicated to creating jobs. In fact, capitalists are constantly devising ways to downsize the workforce. From 1980 to 1990, the net number of jobs created by the biggest corporations in the United States, the "Fortune 500," was zero. The new jobs of that period came mostly from less capital-intensive smaller firms, light industry, service industry, and the public sector.

Since workers are not paid enough to buy back the goods and services they produce, Marx noted, there is always the problem of a disparity between mass production and aggregate demand. If demand slackens, owners cut back on production and investment. Even when there is ample demand, they are tempted to downsize the workforce and intensify the rate of exploitation of the remaining employees, seizing any opportunity to reduce benefits and wages. The ensuing drop in the workforce's buying power leads to a further decline in demand and to business recessions that inflict the greatest pain on those with the least assets.

Marx foresaw this tendency for profits to fall and for protracted recessions and economic instability. As the economist Robert Heilbroner noted, this was an extraordinary prediction, for in Marx's day economists did not recognize boom-and-bust business cycles as inherent to the capitalist system. But today we know that recessions are a chronic condition and—as Marx also predicted—they have become international in scope.

Capital Concentration. When the *Communist Manifesto* first appeared in 1848, bigness was the exception rather than the norm. Yet Marx predicted that large firms would force out or buy up smaller adversaries and increasingly dominate the business world, as capital became more concentrated. This was not the accepted wisdom of that day and must have sounded improbable to those who gave it any attention. But it has come to pass. Indeed, the rate of mergers and take-overs has been higher in the 1980s and 1990s than at any other time in the history of capitalism.

Growth of the Proletariat. Another of Marx's predictions is that the proletariat (workers who have no tools of their own and must work for wages or salaries, selling their labor to someone else) would become an ever-greater percentage of the work force. In 1820 about 75 percent of Americans worked for themselves on farms or in small businesses and artisan crafts. By 1940 that number had dropped to 21.6 percent. Today, less than 10 percent of the labor force is self-employed.

The same shift in the work force can be observed in the Third World. From 1970 to 1980 the number of wage workers in Asia and Africa increased by almost two-thirds, from 72 million to 120 million. The tendency is toward the steady growth of the working class, both industrial and service workers, and—as Marx predicted—this is happening globally, in every land upon which capitalism descends.

Proletarian Revolution. As capitalism develops so will the proletariat, Marx predicted. We have seen that to be true. But he went further: With the growing misery and polarization, the masses would eventually rise up and overthrow the bourgeoisie and put the means of production under public ownership for the benefit of all. The revolution would come in the more industrialized capitalist countries that had large, developed working classes.

What struck Marx about the working class was its level of organization and consciousness. Unlike previously oppressed classes, the proletariat, heavily concentrated in urban areas, seemed capable of an unparalleled level of political development. It would not only rebel against its oppressors as had slaves and serfs but would create an egalitarian, nonexploitative social order as never before seen in history. In his day Marx saw an alternative system emerging in the clubs, mutual aid societies, political organizations, and newspapers of a rapidly growing British working class. For the first time, history would be made by the masses in a conscious way, a class for itself. Sporadic rebellion would be replaced by class-conscious revolution. Instead of burning down the manor, the workers would expropriate it and put it to use for the collective benefit of the common people, the ones who built it in the first place.

Certainly Marx's predictions about revolution have not materialized. There has been no successful proletariat revolution in an advanced capitalist society. As the working class developed so did the capitalist state, whose function has been to protect the capitalist class, with its mechanisms of police suppression and its informational and cultural hegemony.

Of itself, class struggle does not bring inevitable proletarian victory or even a proletarian uprising. Oppressive social conditions may cry out for revolution, but that does not mean revolution is forthcoming. This point is still not understood by some present-day leftists. In his later years, Marx himself began to entertain doubts about the inevitability of a victorious workers revolution. So far, the prevailing force has not been revolution but counterrevolution, the devilish destruction wreaked by capitalist states upon popular struggles, at a cost of millions of lives.

Marx also underestimated the extent to which the advanced capitalist state could use its wealth and power to create a variety of institutions that retard and distract popular consciousness or blunt discontent through reform programs. Contrary to his expectations, successful revolutions occurred in less developed, largely peasant societies such as Russia, China, Cuba, Vietnam—though the proletariats in those countries participated and sometimes, as in the case of Russia in 1917, even spearheaded the insurgency.

Although Marx's predictions about revolution have not materialized as he envisioned, in recent years there have been impressive instances of working-class militancy in South Korea, South Africa, Argentina, Italy, France, Germany, Great Britain, and dozens of other countries, including even the United States. Such mass struggles usually go unreported in the corporate media. In 1984-85, in Great Britain, a bitter, year-long strike resulted in some 10,500 coal miners being arrested, 6,500 injured or battered, and eleven killed. For the British miners locked in that conflict, class struggle was something more than a quaint, obsolete concept.

So in other countries. In Nicaragua, a mass uprising brought down the hated Somoza dictatorship. In Brazil, in 1980-83, as Peter Worsley observes, "the Brazilian working class . . . has played precisely the role assigned to it in 19th century Marxist theory, paralyzing Sao Paulo in a succession of enormous mass strikes that began over bread-and-butter issues but which in the end forced the military to make major political concessions, notably the restoration of a measure of authentic party-political life." Revolutions are relatively rare occurrences but popular struggle is a widespread and constant phenomenon.

More Wealth, More Poverty

Marx believed that as wealth becomes more concentrated, poverty will become more widespread and the plight of working people ever-more desperate. According to his critics, this prediction has proven wrong. They point out that he wrote during a time of raw industrialism, an era of robber barons and the fourteen-hour work day. Through persistent struggle, the working class improved its life conditions from the mid-nineteenth to the mid-twentieth centuries. Today, mainstream spokespersons portray the United States as a prosperous middle-class society.

Yet one might wonder. During the Reagan-Bush-Clinton era, from 1981 to 1996, the share of the national income that went to those who work for a living shrank by over 12 percent. The share that went to those who live off investments increased almost 35 percent. Less than 1 percent of the population owns almost 50 percent of the nation's wealth. The richest families are hundreds of times wealthier than the average household in the lower 90 percent of the population. The gap between America's rich and poor is greater than it has been in more than half a century and is getting ever-greater. Thus, between 1977 and 1989, the top 1 percent saw their earnings grow by over 100 percent, while the three lowest quintiles averaged a 3 to 10 percent drop in real income.[3]

The New York Times (6/20/96) reported that income disparity in 1995 "was wider than it has been since the end of World War II." The average income for the top 20 percent jumped 44 percent, from $73,754 to $105,945, between 1968 and 1994, while the bottom 20

---

[3] Paul Krugman, Peddling Prosperity (New York: W.W. Norton: 1994), 134-35.

percent had a 7 percent increase from $7,202 to $7,762, or only $560 in constant dollars. But these figures understate the problem. The *Times* story is based on a Census Bureau study that fails to report the income of the very rich. For years the reportable upper limit was $300,000 yearly income. In 1994, the bureau lifted the allowable limit to $1 million. This still leaves out the richest one percent, the hundreds of billionaires and thousands of multimillionaires who make many times more than $1 million a year.   The really big money is concentrated in a portion of the population so minuscule as to be judged statistically insignificant. But despite their tiny numbers, the amount of wealth they control is enormous and bespeaks an income disparity a thousand times greater than the spread allowed by the Census Bureau figures. Thus, the difference between a multibillionare who might make $100 million in any one year and a janitor who makes $8,000 is not 14 to 1 (the usually reported spread between highest and lowest) but over 14,000 to 1. Yet the highest incomes remain unreported and uncounted. In a word, most studies of this sort give us no idea of how rich the very rich really are.[4]

The number living below the poverty level in the United States climbed from 24 million in 1977 to over 35 million by 1995. People were falling more deeply into poverty than in earlier times and finding it increasingly difficult to emerge from it. In addition, various diseases related to hunger and poverty have been on the rise.[5]

---

[4] When asked why this procedure was used, a Census Bureau official told my research assistant that the bureau's computers could not handle higher amounts. This excuse seems most improbable, since once the Census Bureau decided to raise the upper limit, it did so without any difficulty. Another reason he gave was confidentiality. Given place coordinates, someone with a very high income could be identified. In addition, high-income respondents understate their income. The interest and dividend earnings they report is only about 50 to 60 percent of actual investment returns. And since their actual numbers are so few, they are likely not to show up in a random sample of the entire nation. By designating the top 20 percent as the "richest," the Census Bureau is lumping in upper-middle professionals and other people who make as little as $70,000 or so, people who are anything but the "richest."

[5] For more extensive data, see my essay "Hidden Holocaust, USA," in Michael Parenti, *Dirty Truths* (San Francisco: City Lights Books, 1996).

There has been a general downgrading of the work force. Regular employment is being replaced by contracted labor or temporary help, resulting in lower wages with fewer or no benefits. Many unions have been destroyed or seriously weakened. Protective government regulations are being rolled back or left unenforced, and there has been an increase in speedups, injuries, and other workplace abuses.

By the 1990s the growing impoverishment of the middle and working classes, including small independent producers, was becoming evident in various countries. In twenty years, more than half the farmers in industrialized countries, some 22 million, were ruined. Meanwhile, as noted in the previous two chapters, free-market "reforms" have brought a dramatic increase in poverty, hunger, crime, and ill-health, along with the growth of large fortunes for the very few in the former communist countries.

The Third World has endured deepening impoverishment over the last half century. As foreign investment has increased, so has the misery of the common people who are driven from the land. Those who manage to find employment in the cities are forced to labor for subsistence wages. We might recall how enclosure acts of the late eighteenth century in England fenced off common lands and drove the peasantry into the industrial hell-holes of Manchester and London, transforming them into beggars or half-starved factory workers. Enclosure continues throughout the Third World, displacing tens of millions of people.

In countries like Argentina, Venezuela, and Peru, per capita income was lower in 1990 than it had been twenty years earlier. In Mexico, workers earned 50 percent less in 1995 than in 1980. One-third of Latin America's population, some 130 million, live in utter destitution, while tens of millions more barely manage. In Brazil, the purchasing power of the lower-income brackets declined by 50 percent between 1940 and 1990 and at least half the population suffered varying degrees of malnutrition.

In much of Africa, misery and hunger have assumed horrendous proportions. In Zaire, 80 percent of the people live in absolute penury. In Asia and Africa more than 40 percent of the population linger at the starvation level. Marx predicted that an expanding capitalism would bring greater wealth for the few and growing misery for the many. That seems to be what is happening—and on a global scale.

A Holistic Science

Repeatedly dismissed as an obsolete "doctrine," Marxism retains a compelling contemporary quality, for it is less a body of fixed dicta and more a method of looking beyond immediate appearances to see the inner qualities and moving forces that shape social relations and much of history itself. As Marx noted: "All science would be superfluous if outward appearances and the essence of things directly coincided." Indeed, perhaps the reason so much of modern social science seems superfluous is because it settles for the tedious tracing of outward appearances.

To understand capitalism, one first has to strip away the appearances presented by its ideology. Unlike most bourgeois theorists, Marx realized that what capitalism claims to be and what it actually is are two different things. What is unique about capitalism is the systematic expropriation of labor for the sole purpose of accumulation. Capital annexes living labor in order to accumulate more capital. The ultimate purpose of work is not to perform services for consumers or sustain life and society, but to make more and more money for the investor irrespective of the human and environmental costs.

An essential point of Marxist analysis is that the social structure and class order prefigure our behavior in many ways. Capitalism moves into every area of work and community, harnessing all of social life to its pursuit of profit. It converts nature, labor, science, art, music, and medicine into commodities and commodities into capital. It transforms land into real estate, folk culture into mass culture, and citizens into debt-ridden workers and consumers.

Marxists understand that a class society is not just a divided society but one ruled by class power, with the state playing the crucial role in maintaining the existing class structure. Marxism might be considered a "holistic" science in that it recognizes the links between various components of the social system. Capitalism is not just an economic system but a political and cultural one as well, an entire social order. When we study any part of that order, be it the news or entertainment media, criminal justice, Congress, defense spending, overseas military intervention, intelligence agencies, campaign finance, science and technology, education, medical care, taxation, transportation, housing, or whatever, we will see how the particular part reflects the nature of the whole. Its unique dynamic often buttresses and is shaped by the larger social system—especially the system's overriding need to maintain the prerogatives of the corporate class.

In keeping with their system-sustaining function, the major news media present reality as a scatter of events and subjects that ostensibly bear little relation to each other or to a larger set of social relations. Consider a specific phenomenon like racism. Racism is presented as essentially a set of bad attitudes held by racists. There is little analysis of what makes it so functional for a class society. Instead, race and class are treated as mutually exclusive concepts in competition with each other. But those who have an understanding of class power know that as class contradictions deepen and come to the fore, racism becomes not less but more important as a factor in class conflict. In short, both race and class are likely to be crucial arenas of struggle at the very same time.

Marxists further maintain that racism involves not just personal attitude but institutional structure and systemic power. They point out that racist organizations and sentiments are often propagated by well-financed reactionary forces seeking to divide the working populace against itself, fracturing it into antagonistic ethnic enclaves.

Marxists also point out that racism is used as a means of depressing wages by keeping a segment of the labor force vulnerable to super-exploitation. To see racism in the larger context of corporate society is to move from a liberal complaint to a radical analysis. Instead of thinking that racism is an irrational output of a basically rational and benign system, we should see it is a rational output of a basically irrational and unjust system. By "rational" I mean purposive and functional in sustaining the system that nurtures it.

Lacking a holistic approach to society, conventional social science tends to compartmentalize social experience. So we are asked to ponder whether this or that phenomenon is cultural or economic or psychological, when usually it is a blend of all these things. Thus, an automobile is unmistakably an economic artifact but it also has a cultural and psychological component, and even an aesthetic dimension. We need a greater sense of how analytically distinct phenomena are often empirically interrelated and may actually gather strength and definition from each other.

Marxists do not accept the prevalent view of institutions as just "being there," with all the natural innocence of mountains—especially the more articulated formal institutions such as the church, army, police, military, university, media, medicine, and the like. Institutions are heavily shaped by class interests and class power. Far from being neutral and independent bastions, the major institutions of society are tied to the big business class. Corporate representatives exercise direct decision-making power through control of governing boards and directorships. Business elites usually control the budgets and the very property of various institutions, a control inscribed into law through corporate charters and enforced by the police powers of the state. Their power extends to the managers picked, the policies set, and the performances of employees.

If conventional social science has any one dedication, it is to ignore the linkages between social action and the systemic demands of capitalism, avoiding any view of power in its class dimensions, and any view of class as a power relationship. For conventional researchers, power is seen as fragmented and fluid, and class is nothing more than an occupational or income category to be correlated with voting habits, consumer styles or whatever, and not as a relationship between those who own and those who labor for those who own.

In the Marxist view there can be no such thing as a class as such, a social entity unto itself. There can be no lords without serfs, no masters without slaves, no capitalists without workers. More than just a sociological category, class is a relationship to the means of production and to social and state power. This idea, so fundamental to an understanding of public policy, is avoided by conventional social scientists who prefer to concentrate on everything else but class power realities.[6]

It is remarkable, for instance, that some political scientists have studied the presidency and Congress for decades without uttering a word about capitalism, without so much as a sidelong glance at how the imperatives of a capitalist politico-economic order play such a crucial role in prefiguring the political agenda. Social science is cluttered with "community power studies" that treat communities and issues as isolated autonomous entities. Such investigations are usually limited to the immediate interplay of policy actors, with little said about how issues link up to a larger range of social interests.

Conservative ideological preconceptions regularly influence the research strategies of most social scientists and policy analysts. In political science, for instance:

(1) The relationships between industrial capitalist nations and Third World nations are described as (a) "dependency" and "interdependency" and as fostering a mutually beneficial development, rather than (b) an imperialism that exploits the land, labor, and

---

[6] See the discussion on class in the following chapter.

resources of weaker nations for the benefit of the favored classes in both the industrial and less-developed worlds.

(2) The United States and other "democratic capitalist" societies are said to be held together by (a) common values that reflect the common interest, not by (b) class power and domination.

(3) The fragmentation of power in the political process is supposedly indicative of (a) a fluidity and democratization of interest-group pluralism, rather than (b) the pocketing and structuring of power in unaccountable and undemocratic ways.

(4) The mass propagation of conventional political beliefs is described as (a) political "socialization" and "education for citizenship," and is treated as a desirable civic process, rather than (b) an indoctrination that distorts the information flow and warps the public's critical perceptions.

In each of these instances, mainstream academics offer version *a* not as a research finding but as an a priori assumption that requires no critical analysis, upon which research is then predicated. At the same time they disregard the evidence and research that supports version *b*.

By ignoring the dominant class conditions that exercise such an influence over social behavior, conventional social science can settle on surface factualness, trying to explain immediate actions in exclusively immediate terms. Such an approach places a high priority on epiphenomenal and idiosyncratic explanations, the peculiarities of specific personalities and situations. What is habitually overlooked in such research (and in our news reports, our daily observations, and sometimes even our political struggles) is the way seemingly remote forces may prefigure our experiences.

Learning to Ask Why

When we think without Marx's perspective, that is, without considering class interests and class power, we seldom ask *why* certain things happen. Many things are reported in the news but few are explained. Little is said about how the social order is organized and whose interests prevail. Devoid of a framework that explains why things happen, we are left to see the world as do mainstream media pundits: as a flow of events, a scatter of particular developments and personalities unrelated to a larger set of social relations—propelled by happenstance, circumstance, confused intentions, and individual ambition, never by powerful class interests—and yet producing effects that serve such interests with impressive regularity.

Thus we fail to associate social problems with the socio-economic forces that create them and we learn to truncate our own critical thinking. Imagine if we attempted something different; for example, if we tried to explain that wealth and poverty exist together not in accidental juxtaposition, but because wealth causes poverty, an inevitable outcome of economic exploitation both at home and abroad. How could such an analysis gain any exposure in the capitalist media or in mainstream political life?

Suppose we started with a particular story about how child labor in Indonesia is contracted by multinational corporations at near-starvation wage levels. This information probably would not be carried in rightwing publications, but in 1996 it did appear—after decades of effort by some activists—in the centrist mainstream press. What if we then crossed a line and said that these exploitative employer-employee relations were backed by the full might of the Indonesian military government. Fewer media would carry this story but it still might get mentioned in an inside page of the *New York Times* or *Washington Post*.

Then suppose we crossed another line and said that these repressive arrangements would not prevail were it not for generous military aid from the United States, and that for almost thirty years the homicidal Indonesian military has been financed, armed, advised, and trained by the U.S. national security state. Such a story would be even more unlikely to appear in the liberal press but it is still issue-specific and safely without an overall class analysis, so it might well make its way into left-liberal opinion publications like the *Nation* and the *Progressive*.

Now suppose we pointed out that the conditions found in Indonesia—the heartless economic exploitation, brutal military repression, and lavish U.S. support—exist in scores of other countries. Suppose we then crossed that most serious line of all and instead of just deploring this fact we also asked *why* successive U.S. administrations involve themselves in such unsavory pursuits throughout the world. And what if then we tried to explain that the whole phenomenon is consistent with the U.S. dedication to making the world safe for the free market and the giant multinational corporations, and that the intended goals are (a) to maximize opportunities to accumulate wealth by depressing the wage levels of workers throughout the world and preventing them from organizing on behalf of their own interests, and (b) to protect the overall global system of free-market capital accumulation.

Then what if, from all this, we concluded that U.S. foreign policy is neither timid, as the conservatives say, nor foolish, as the liberals say, but is remarkably successful in rolling back just about all governments and social movements that attempt to serve popular needs rather than private corporate greed.

Such an analysis, hurriedly sketched here, would take some effort to lay out and would amount to a Marxist critique—a correct critique—of capitalist imperialism. Though Marxists are not the only ones that might arrive at it, it almost certainly would not be published anywhere except in a Marxist publication. We crossed too many lines. Because we tried to explain the particular situation (child labor) in terms of a larger set of social relations (corporate class power), our presentation would be rejected out of hand as "ideological." The perceptual taboos imposed by the dominant powers teach people to avoid thinking critically about such powers. In contrast, Marxism gets us into the habit of asking why, of seeing the linkage between political events and class power.

A common method of devaluing Marxism is to misrepresent what it actually says and then attack the misrepresentation. This happens easily enough since most of the anti-Marxist critics and their audiences have only a passing familiarity with Marxist literature and rely instead on their own caricatured notions. Thus, the Roman Catholic *Pastoral Letter on Marxist Communism* rejects the claim that "structural [read, class] revolution can entirely cure a disease that is man himself" nor can it provide "the solution of all human suffering." But who makes such a claim? There is no denying that revolution does not entirely cure all human suffering. But why is that assertion used as a refutation of Marxism? Most Marxists are neither chiliastic nor utopian. They dream not of a perfect society but of a better, more just life. They make no claim to eliminating all suffering, and recognize that even in the best of societies there are the inevitable assaults of misfortune, mortality, and other vulnerabilities of life. And certainly in any society there are some people who, for whatever reason, are given to wrongful deeds and self-serving corruptions. The highly imperfect nature of human beings should make us all the more determined not to see power and wealth accumulating in the hands of an unaccountable few, which is the central dedication of capitalism.

Capitalism and its various institutions affect the most personal dimensions of everyday life in ways not readily evident. A Marxist approach helps us to see connections to which we were previously blind, to relate effects to causes, and to replace the arbitrary and the mysterious with the regular and the necessary. A Marxist perspective helps us to see injustice as rooted in systemic causes that go beyond individual choice, and to view crucial developments not as neutral happenings but as the intended consequences of class power and interest. Marxism also shows how even *un*intended consequences can be utilized by those with superior resources to service their interests.

Is Marx still relevant today? Only if you want to know why the media distort the news in a mostly mainstream direction; why more and more people at home and abroad face economic adversity while money continues to accumulate in the hands of relatively few; why there is so much private wealth and public poverty in this country and elsewhere; why U.S. forces find it necessary to intervene in so many regions of the world; why a rich and productive economy offers chronic recessions, underemployment, and neglect of social needs; and why many political officeholders are unwilling or unable to serve the public interest.[7]

Some Marxist theorists have so ascended into the numbing altitudes of abstract cogitation that they seldom touch political realities here on earth. They spend their time talking to each other in self-referential code, a scholastic ritual that Doug Dowd described as "How many Marxists can dance on the head of a surplus value." Fortunately there are others who not only *tell* us about Marxist theory but *demonstrate* its utility by applying it to political actualities. They know how to draw connections between immediate experience and the larger structural forces that shape that experience. They cross the forbidden line and talk about class power.

This is why, for all the misrepresentation and suppression, Marxist scholarship survives. While not having all the answers, it does have a superior explanatory power, telling us something about reality that bourgeois scholarship refuses to do. Marxism offers the kind of subversive truths that cause fear and trembling among the high and mighty, those who live atop a mountain of lies.

---

[7] To further pursue these questions, the reader is invited to read several of my books: *Democracy for the Few*, 6th edition, (New York: St. Martin's Press, 1995); *Against Empire* (San Francisco: City Lights Books, 1995); and *Dirty Truths* (San Francisco: City Lights Books, 1996).

CHAPTER 9

ANYTHING BUT CLASS: AVOIDING THE C-WORD

"Class" is a concept that is strenuously avoided by both mainstream writers and many on the Left. When certain words are eliminated from public discourse, so are certain thoughts. Dissident ideas become all the more difficult to express when there are no words to express them. "Class" is usually dismissed as an outworn Marxist notion with no relevance to contemporary society. It is a five-letter word that is treated like a dirty four-letter one.

With the C-word out of the way, it is then easy to dispose of other politically unacceptable concepts such as class privilege, class power, class exploitation, class interest, and class struggle. These too are judged no longer relevant, if ever they were, in a society that supposedly consists of the fluid pluralistic interplay of diverse groups.

The Class Denial of Class

Those who occupy the higher circles of wealth and power are keenly aware of their own interests. While they sometimes seriously differ among themselves on specific issues, they exhibit an impressive cohesion when it comes to protecting the existing class system of corporate power, property, privilege, and profit.

At the same time, they are careful to discourage public awareness of the class power they wield. They avoid the C-word, especially when used in reference to themselves as in "owning class," "upper class," or "moneyed class." And they like it least when the politically active elements of the owning class are called the "ruling class."

The ruling class in this country has labored long to leave the impression that it does not exist, does not own the lion's share of just about everything, and does not exercise a vastly disproportionate influence over the affairs of the nation. Such precautions are themselves symptomatic of an acute awareness of class interests.

Yet ruling class members are far from invisible. Their command positions in the corporate world, their control of international finance and industry, their ownership of the major media, and their influence over state power and the political process are all matters of public record—to some limited degree.[1] While it would seem a simple matter to apply the C-word to those who occupy the highest reaches of the C-world, the dominant class ideology dismisses any such application as a lapse into "conspiracy theory."

The C-word is also taboo when applied to the millions who do the work of society for what are usually niggardly wages, the "working class," a term that is dismissed as Marxist jargon. And it is verboten to refer to the "exploiting and exploited classes," for then one is talking about the very essence of the capitalist system, the accumulation of corporate wealth at the expense of labor.

The C-word is an acceptable term when prefaced with the soothing adjective "middle." Every politician, publicist, and pundit will rhapsodize about the *middle* class, the object of their heartfelt concern. The much admired and much pitied middle class is suppos-

---

[1] For a more detailed treatment of ruling-class resources and influences, see my *Democracy for the Few*, 6th edition (New York: St. Martin's Press, 1995).

edly inhabited by virtuously self-sufficient people, free from the presumed profligacy of those who inhabit the lower rungs of society. By including almost everyone, "middle class" serves as a conveniently amorphous concept that masks the exploitation and inequality of social relations. It is a class label that denies the actuality of class power.

The C-word is allowable when applied to one other group, the desperate lot who live on the lowest rung of society, who get the least of everything while being regularly blamed for their own victimization: the "underclass." References to the presumed deficiencies of underclass people are acceptable because they reinforce the existing social hierarchy and justify the unjust treatment accorded society's most vulnerable elements.

Class reality is obscured by an ideology whose tenets might be summarized and rebutted as follows:

Credo: There are no real class divisions in this society. Save for some rich and poor, almost all of us are middle class.

Response: Wealth is enormously concentrated in the hands of relatively few in this country, while tens of millions work for poverty-level wages, when work is to be had. The gap between rich and poor has always been great and has been growing since the late 1970s. Those in the middle also have been enduring increasing economic injustice and insecurity.

Credo: Our social institutions and culture are autonomous entities in a pluralistic society, largely free of the influences of wealth and class power. To think otherwise is to entertain conspiracy theories.

Response: Great concentrations of wealth exercise an influence in all aspects of life, often a dominating one. Our social and cultural institutions are run by boards of directors (or trustees or regents) drawn largely from interlocking, nonelective, self-selecting corporate elites. They and their faithful hirelings occupy most of the command positions of the executive state and other policymaking bodies, and manifest a keen awareness of their class interests when shaping domestic and international policies. This includes such policies as the General Agreement on Tariffs and Trade (GATT), designed to circumvent whatever democratic sovereignty exists within nations.[2]

Credo: The differences between rich and poor are a natural given, not causally linked. Individual human behavior, not class, determines human performance and life chances. Existing social arrangements are a natural reflection of largely innate human proclivities.

Response: All conservative ideologies justify existing inequities as the natural order of things, inevitable outcomes of human nature. If the very rich are naturally so much more capable than the rest of us, why must they be provided with so many artificial privileges under the law, so many bailouts, subsidies, and other special considerations—at our expense? Their "naturally superior talents" include unprincipled and illegal subterfuges such as price-fixing, stock manipulation, insider trading, fraud, tax evasion, the legal enforcement of unfair competition, ecological spoliation, harmful products, and unsafe work conditions. One might expect naturally superior people not to act in such rapacious and venal ways. Differences in talent and capacity as might exist between individuals do not excuse the crimes and injustices that are endemic to the corporate business system.

The ABC Theorists

Even among persons normally identified as progressive, one finds a reluctance to deal with the reality of capitalist class power. Sometimes the dismissal of the C-word is quite categorical. At a meeting in New York in 1986 I heard the sociologist Stanley Aronowitz comment, "When I hear the word 'class' I just yawn." For Aronowitz, class is a concept of diminishing importance used by

---

[2] For a discussion of GATT see my *Against Empire* (San Francisco: City Lights Books, 1995).

those he repeatedly referred to as "orthodox Marxists."[3]

Another left academic, Ronald Aronson, in a book entitled *After Marxism*, claims—in the face of all recent evidence—that classes in capitalist society have become "less polarized" and class exploitation is not an urgent issue nowadays because labor unions "have achieved power to protect their members and affect social policy." This at a time when many unions are being destroyed, workers are being downgraded to the status of contract laborers, and the income gap is wider than in decades.

Many who pretend to be on the Left are so rabidly anti-Marxist as to seize upon any conceivable notion except class power to explain what is happening in the world. They are the Anything-But-Class (ABC) theorists who, while not allied with conservatives on most

---

[3] Aronowitz and some other "left" academics do battle against Marxism by producing hypertheorized exegeses in a field called "cultural studies." That their often impenetrable writings seldom connect to the real world was demonstrated in 1996 by physicist Alan Sokal, himself a leftist, who wrote a cultural studies parody and submitted it to Aronowitz's *Social Text*, a journal devoted to articles that specialize in bloated verbiage, pedantic pretensions, and academic one-upmanship. Sokal's piece was laden with obscure but trendy jargon and footnoted references to the likes of Jacques Derrida and Aronowitz himself. It purported to be an "epistemic exposition" of "recent developments in quantum gravity" and "the space-time manifold" and "foundational conceptual categories of prior science" that have "become problematized and relativized" with "profound implications for the content of a future post-modern and liberatory science." Various *Social Text* editors read and accepted the piece as a serious contribution. After they published it, Sokal revealed that it was little more than fabricated gibberish that "wasn't obliged to respect any standards of evidence or logic." In effect, he demonstrated that the journal's editors were themselves so profoundly immersed in pretentiously inflated discourse as to be unable to distinguish between a genuine intellectual effort and a silly parody. Aronowitz responded by calling Sokal "ill-read and half-educated" (*New York Times*, 5/18/96).

One is reminded of Robert McChesney's comment: "At some universities the very term cultural studies has become an ongoing punchline to a bad joke. It signifies half-assed research, self-congratulation, and farcical pretension. At its worst, the proponents of this newfangled cultural studies are unable to defend their work, so they no longer try, merely claiming that their critics are hung up on outmoded notions like evidence, logic, science, and rationality" (*Monthly Review*, 3/96). In my opinion, one of the main effects of cultural studies is to draw attention away from the vital realities of class power, the "outmoded" things that cause Aronowitz and his associates to yawn.

political issues, do their part in stunting class consciousness.[4]

The "left" ABC theorists say we are giving too much attention to class. Who exactly is doing that? Surveying the mainstream academic publications, radical journals, and socialist scholars conferences, one is hard put to find much class analysis of any kind. Far from giving too much attention to class power, most U.S. writers and commentators have yet to discover the subject. While pummeling a rather minuscule Marxist Left, the ABC theorists would have us think they are doing courageous battle against hordes of Marxists who dominate intellectual discourse in this country—yet another hallucination they hold in common with conservatives.[5]

In their endless search for conceptual schema that might mute Marxism's class analysis, "left" ABC theorists have twaddled for years over a false dichotomization between early Marx (culturalistic, humanistic, good) and later Marx (dogmatic, economistic, bad).[6] As

---

[4] For prime examples, try the bloated, pretentious prose of such left anticommunist theorists as Ernesto Laclau and Chantal Mouffe, both of whom are treated reverently by their counterparts in this country. One recent fad of the "left" ABC intellectuals is "post-modernism," which argues that the principles of rationality and evidence of modern times no longer apply; longstanding ideologies have lost their relevance as has most of political economy and history; and one cannot hope to develop a reliable critique of class and institutional forces. While claiming to search for new "meanings," post-modernism resembles the same old anti-class theories, both right and left. For a discussion and critique, see Ellen Meiksins Wood and John Bellamy Foster (eds.), *In Defense of History* (New York: Monthly Review Press, 1977).

[5] Some publications that claim to be on the Left, such as *Dissent, New Republic, New Politics, Telos, In These Times,* and *Democratic Left* can often be as unyielding as any conservative rag in their anticommunism, anti-Marxism, and of course anti-Sovietism.

[6] One of those who pretends to be on the Left is John Judis, whose impressive illiteracy in regard to Marxism does not prevent him from distinguishing between "humanistic" Marxists and Marxists who are "simple-minded economic determinists" (*In These Times,* 9/23/81). According to Judis, the latter fail to ascribe any importance to cultural conditions and political structures. I know of no Marxists who fit that description. I, for one, treat cultural and political institutions in much detail in various books of mine—but culture as anchored in an overall system of corporate ownership and control; see my *Power and the Powerless* (New York: St. Martin's Press, 1978); *Make-Believe Media: The Politics of Entertainment* (New York: St. Martin's Press, 1992); *Inventing Reality: The Politics of News Media,*

Marxist scholar Bertell Ollman notes, this artificial counterpoising transforms a relatively minor development in Marx's work into a chasm between two ways of thinking that have little in common.[7]

Some ABC theorists labored hard to promote the writings of the late Italian Communist party leader Antonio Gramsci as a source of cultural theory to counteract a Marxist class analysis. (See, for instance, publications like Paul Piccone's *Telos* during the 1970s and early 1980s.) Gramsci, they said, rejected the "economistic" views of Marx and Lenin and did not treat class conflict as a central concept, preferring to develop a more "nuanced analysis" based on cultural hegemony. So Gramsci was made into "the Marxist who's safe to bring home to Mother," as the historian T.J. Jackson put it. And as Christopher Phelps added:

> Gramsci has become safe, tame, denatured—a wisp of his revolutionary self. Academics seeking to justify their retreat into highly abstruse theories have created fanciful illusions about their 'counter-hegemonic' activity. They have created a mythical Gramsci who holds views he never did, including an opposition to revolutionary socialist organization of the sort that he, following upon Lenin, held indispensable" (*Monthly Review*, 11/95).

Gramsci himself would have considered the representations made about him by ABC theorists as oddly misplaced. He never treated culture and class as mutually exclusive terms but saw cultural hegemony as a vital instrument of the ruling class. Furthermore, he occu-

---

2nd edition (New York: St. Martin's Press, 1993); *Land of Idols: Political Mythology in America* (New York: St. Martin's Press, 1994 and *Dirty Truths* (San Francisco: City Lights Books, 1996).

[7] Ollman points out that Marx's analytic framework did not emerge from his head full blown. In the earlier works, such as the *Economic and Philosophic Manuscripts* and *The German Ideology*, Marx is in the process of becoming a Marxist and is piecing together his understanding of capitalism in history, leaning more heavily on his philosophical training and his criticisms of the neo-Hegelians. Though more prevalent in the earlier writings, concepts such as alienation and the language of dialectics appear throughout his work, including *Capital*; see Bertell Ollman's forthcoming article, "The Myth of the Two Marxs"; also David McLellan, *The Young Hegelians and Karl Marx* (London: McMillan: 1969).

pied a prominent position of responsibility in the Italian Communist party and considered himself firmly within the Marxist-Leninist camp.

To the extent that class is accorded any attention in academic social science, pop sociology, and media commentary, it is as a kind of demographic trait or occupational status. So sociologists refer to "upper-middle," "lower-middle," and the like. Reduced to a demographic trait, one's class affiliation certainly can seem to have relatively low political salience. Society itself becomes little more than a pluralistic configuration of status groups. Class is not a taboo subject if divorced from capitalism's exploitative accumulation process.

Both mainstream social scientists and "left" ABC theorists fail to consider the dynamic interrelationship that gives classes their significance. In contrast, Marxists treat class as the key concept in an entire social order known as capitalism (or feudalism or slavery), centering around the ownership of the means of production (factories, mines, oil wells, agribusinesses, media conglomerates, and the like) and the need—if one lacks ownership—to sell one's labor on terms that are highly favorable to the employer.

Class gets its significance from the process of surplus extraction. The relationship between worker and owner is essentially an exploitative one, involving the constant transfer of wealth from those who labor (but do not own) to those who own (but do not labor). This is how some people get richer and richer without working, or with doing only a fraction of the work that enriches them, while others toil hard for an entire lifetime only to end up with little or nothing.

Both orthodox social scientists and "left" ABC theorists treat the diverse social factions within the noncapitalist class as classes unto themselves; so they speak of a "blue-collar class," a "professional class," and the like. In doing so, they claim to be moving beyond a "reductionist," Marxist dualistic model of classes. But what is more reductionist than to ignore the underlying dynamics of economic power and the conflict between capital and labor? What is more misleading than to treat occupational groups as autonomous classes, giving attention to every social group in capitalist society except the capitalist class itself, to every social conflict except class conflict?

Both conventional and "left" ABC theorists have difficulty understanding that the creation of a managerial or technocratic social formation constitutes no basic change in the property relations of capitalism, no creation of new classes. Professionals and managers are not an autonomous class as such. Rather they are mental workers who live much better than most other employees but who still serve the accumulation process on behalf of corporate owners.

Everyday Class Struggle

To support their view that class (in the Marxist sense) is passé, the ABC theorists repeatedly assert that there is not going to be a workers' revolution in the United States in the foreseeable future. (I heard this sentiment expressed at three different panels during a "Gramsci conference" at Amherst, Massachusetts, in April 1987.) Even if we agree with this prophecy, we might still wonder how it becomes grounds for rejecting class analysis and for concluding that there is no such thing as exploitation of labor by capital and no opposition from people who work for a living.

The feminist revolution that was going to transform our entire patriarchal society has thus far not materialized, yet no progressive person takes this to mean that sexism is a chimera or that gender-related struggles are of no great moment. That workers in the United States are not throwing up barricades does not mean class struggle is a myth. In present-day society, such struggle permeates almost all workplace activities. Employers are relentlessly grinding away at workers and workers are constantly fighting back against employers.

Capital's class war is waged with court injunctions, antilabor laws, police repression, union busting, contract violations, sweatshops, dishonest clocking of time, safety violations, harassment and firing of resistant workers, cutbacks in wages and benefits, raids of pension funds, layoffs, and plant closings. Labor fights back with union organizing, strikes, slowdowns, boycotts, public demonstrations, job actions, coordinated absenteeism, and workplace sabotage.

Class has a dynamic that goes beyond its immediate visibility. Whether we are aware of it or not, class realities permeate our society, determining much about our capacity to pursue our own interests. Class power is a factor in setting the political agenda, selecting leaders, reporting the news, funding science and education, distributing health care, mistreating the environment, depressing wages, resisting racial and gender equality, marketing entertainment and the arts, propagating religious messages, suppressing dissidence, and defining social reality itself.

ABC theorists see the working class as not only incapable of revolution but as on the way out, declining in significance as a social formation.[8] Anyone who still thinks that class is of primary importance is labeled a diehard Marxist, guilty of "economism" and "reductionism" and unable to keep up with the "post-Marxist," "post-structuralist," "post-industrialist," "post-capitalist," "post-modernist," and "post-deconstructionist" times.

It is ironic that some left intellectuals should deem class struggle to be largely irrelevant at the very time class power is becoming increasingly transparent, at the very time corporate concentration and profit accumulation is more rapacious than ever, and the tax system has become more regressive and oppressive, the upward transfer of income and wealth has accelerated, public sector assets are being privatized, corporate money exercises an increasing control over the political process, people at home and abroad are working harder for less, and throughout the world poverty is growing at a faster rate than overall population.

There are neo-conservatives and mainstream centrists who man-

---

[8] Most ABC theorists have very limited day-to-day experience with actual working people, a fact that may contribute to their impression that the working class is of marginal import.

ifest a better awareness of class struggle than the "left" ABC theorists. Thus former managing editor of the *New York Times* A. M.
Rosenthal sees the Republican party's "slash and burn" offensive
against social programs as "not only a prescription for class struggle
but the beginning of its reality" (*New York Times*, 3/21/95).
Rosenthal goes on to quote Wall Street financier Felix Rohatyn who
notes that "the big beneficiaries of our economic expansion have
been the owners of financial assets" in what amounts to "a huge
transfer of wealth from lower-skilled middle-class American workers to the owners of capital assets and to the new technological aristocracy." Increasingly, "working people see themselves as simply
temporary assets to be hired or fired to protect the bottom line and
create 'shareholder value.' "

It says little for "left" ABC intellectuals when they can be out-
classed by establishment people like Rosenthal and Rohatyn.

Seizing upon anything but class, U.S. leftists today have developed
an array of identity groups centering around ethnic, gender, cultural,
and life-style issues. These groups treat their respective grievances as
something apart from class struggle, and have almost nothing to say
about the increasingly harsh politico-economic *class* injustices perpetrated against us all. Identity groups tend to emphasize their distinc-
tiveness and their separateness from each other, thus fractionalizing
the protest movement. To be sure, they have important contributions
to make around issues that are particularly salient to them, issues
often overlooked by others. But they also should not downplay their
common interests, nor overlook the common class enemy they face.
The forces that impose class injustice and economic exploitation are
the same ones that propagate racism, sexism, militarism, ecological
devastation, homophobia, xenophobia, and the like.

People may not develop a class consciousness but they still are
affected by the power, privileges, and handicaps related to the distribution of wealth and want. These realities are not canceled out by
race, gender, or culture. The latter factors operate within an overall

class society. The exigencies of class power and exploitation shape the social reality we all live in. Racism and sexism help to create superexploited categories of workers (minorities and women) and reinforce the notions of inequality that are so functional for a capitalist system.

To embrace a class analysis is not to deny the significance of identity issues but to see how these are linked both to each other and to the overall structure of politico-economic power. An awareness of class relations deepens our understanding of culture, race, gender, and other such things.

Wealth and Power

In order that a select few might live in great opulence, millions of people work hard for an entire lifetime, never free from financial insecurity, and at great cost to the quality of their lives. The complaint is not that the very rich have so much more than everyone else but that their superabundance and endless accumulation comes at the expense of everyone and everything else, including our communities and our environment.

Great concentrations of wealth give the owning class control not only over the livelihoods of millions but over civic life itself. Money is the necessary ingredient that gives the rich their immense political influence, their monopoly ownership of mass media, their access to skilled lobbyists and high public office. To those who possess it, great wealth also brings social prestige and cultural dominance, including membership on the governing boards of foundations, universities, museums, research institutions, and professional schools.

Likewise, the absence of money is what makes the have-nots and have-littles relatively powerless, depriving them of access to national media and severely limiting their influence over political decision-makers. As the gap between the corporate rich and the rest of us grows, the opportunities for popular rule diminish.

There is much discourse on "how to balance freedom with security." History offers numerous examples of leaders who in the name of national security have been ready to extinguish what precious few liberties people might have won after generations of struggle. Challenges to the privileged social order are treated as attacks upon all social order, a plunge into chaos and anarchy. Repressive measures are declared necessary to safeguard people from the dangers of terrorists, subversives, Reds, and other supposed enemies, both foreign and domestic.

Again and again we are asked to choose between freedom and security when in truth there is no security without freedom. In both dictatorships and democracies, the agencies of "national security," acting secretively and unaccountably, have regularly violated both our freedom and our security, practicing every known form of repression, corruption, and deceit.

Once in control of the state, plutocratic interests can use a regressive taxation system to make the public pay for the agencies of repression that are essential to elite domination. Still, democratic governance can prove troublesome, inciting all sorts of popular demands and imposing restraints on Big Business's enjoyment of a freewheeling market. For this reason the captains of capitalism and their conservative publicists support both a strong state armed with every intrusive power and a weak government unable to stop corporate abuse or serve the needs of the ordinary populace.

Aside from the systemic imperatives that cause capitalism to accumulate without end, we must also reckon with the driving force of class greed. Wealth is an addiction. There is no end to the amount of money one might desire to accumulate. The best security to being rich is to get still richer, piling possession upon possession, giving oneself over to the *auri sacra fames,* the cursed greed for gold, the desire for more money than can be consumed in a thousand lifetimes of limitless indulgence, wanting in nothing but still more and more money.

Wealth buys every comfort and privilege in life, the fame of fortune, elevating the possessor to the highest social stratosphere, an
expression of the aggrandizing self, an expansion of the ego's bound-
ary, an extension of one's existence beyond the grave, leaving one
feeling almost invulnerable to time and mortality.

Wealth is pursued without moral restraint. The very rich try to
crush anyone who resists their endless, heartless, unprincipled accumulation. Like any addiction, money is pursued in that obsessive,
amoral, singleminded way, revealing a total disregard for what is
right or wrong, just or unjust, an indifference to other considerations
and other people's interests—and even one's own interests should
they go beyond feeding the addiction.[9]

Capitalism is a rational system, the well-calculated systematic
maximization of power and profits, a process of accumulation
anchored in material obsession that has the ultimately irrational consequence of devouring the system itself—and everything else with it.

Eco-Apocalypse, a Class Act

In 1876, Marx's collaborator, Frederich Engels, offered a prophetic
caveat: "Let us not . . . flatter ourselves overmuch on account of our
human conquest over nature. For each such conquest takes its
revenge on us. . . . At every step we are reminded that we by no means
rule over nature like a conqueror over a foreign people, like someone
standing outside of nature—but that we, with flesh, blood, and
brain, belong to nature, and exist in its midst. . . ."

With its never-ending emphasis on exploitation and expansion,
and its indifference to environmental costs, capitalism appears determined to stand outside nature. The essence of capitalism, its raison

---

[9] Thus it is necessary and desirable to have laws to protect the environment,
workers' lives, and consumer health because big business has a total indifference
to such things, and—to the extent that they cut into profits—an outright
hostility toward regulations on behalf of the public interest. We sometimes
forget how profoundly immoral is corporate power.

d'être, is to convert nature into commodities and commodities into capital, transforming the living earth into inanimate wealth. This capital accumulation process wreaks havoc upon the global ecological system. It treats the planet's life-sustaining resources (arable land, groundwater, wetlands, forests, fisheries, ocean beds, rivers, air quality) as dispensable ingredients of limitless supply, to be consumed or toxified at will. Consequently, the support systems of the entire ecosphere—the planet's thin skin of fresh air, water, and top soil—are at risk, threatened by such things as global warming, massive erosion, and ozone depletion.

Global warming is caused by tropical deforestation, motor vehicle exhaust, and other fossil fuel emissions that create a "greenhouse effect," trapping heat close to the earth's surface. This massed heat is altering the atmospheric chemistry and climatic patterns across the planet, causing record droughts, floods, tidal waves, snow storms, hurricanes, heat waves, and great losses in soil moisture. We now know that the planet does not have a limitless ability to absorb heat caused by energy consumption.

Another potential catastrophe is the shrinkage of the ozone layer that shields us from the sun's deadliest rays. Over 2.5 billion pounds of ozone-depleting chemicals are emitted into the earth's atmosphere every year, resulting in excessive ultraviolet radiation that is causing an alarming rise in skin cancer and other diseases. Increased radiation is damaging trees, crops, and coral reefs, and destroying the ocean's phytoplankton—source of about half of the planet's oxygen. If the oceans die, so do we.

At the same time, the rise in pollution and population has given us acid rain, soil erosion, silting of waterways, shrinking grasslands, disappearing water supplies and wetlands, and the obliteration of thousands of species, with hundreds more on the endangered list.[10]

---

[10] Putting an end to the population explosion will not of itself save the ecosphere but *not* ending it will add greatly to the dangers the planet faces. The environment can sustain a quality life for just so many people.

In 1970, on what was called "Environment Day," President Richard Nixon intoned: "What a strange creature is man that he fouls his own nest." With that utterance, Nixon was helping to propagate the myth that the ecological crisis we face is a matter of irrational individual behavior rather than being of a social magnitude. In truth, the problem is not individual choice but the system that imposes itself on individuals and prefigures their choice. Behind the ecological crisis is the reality of class interest and power.

An ever-expanding capitalism and a fragile, finite ecology are on a calamitous collision course. It is not true that the ruling politico-economic interests are in a state of denial about this. Far worse than denial, they are in a state of utter antagonism toward those who think the planet is more important than corporate profits. So they defame environmentalists as "eco-terrorists," "EPA gestapo," "Earth Day alarmists," "tree huggers," and purveyors of "Green hysteria" and "liberal claptrap."

Some environmental activists in this country have been the object of terrorist assaults conducted by unknown assailants, with the implicit tolerance of law enforcement authorities.[11] Autocrats in countries like Nigeria, in bed with the polluting oil companies, have waged brutal war upon environmentalists, going so far as to hang popular leader Ken Saro Wiwa.

In recent years, conservatives within and without Congress, fueled by corporate lobbyists, have supported measures that would (1) prevent the Environmental Protection Agency from keeping toxic fill out of lakes and harbors, (2) eliminate most of the wetland acreage that was to be set aside for a reserve, (3) completely deregulate the

---

[11] To offer one example: the FBI was quick to make arrests when environmentalists Judi Bari and Darryl Cherney were seriously injured by a car bomb in 1990. They arrested Bari and Cherney, calling them "radical activists," charging that the bomb must have belonged to them. Both have long been outspoken advocates of nonviolence. The charges were eventually dropped for lack of evidence. (The bomb had been planted under the driver's seat.) The FBI named no other suspects and did no real investigation of the attack.

production of chlorofluorocarbons that deplete the ozone layer, (4) virtually eliminate clean water and clean air standards, (5) open the unspoiled Arctic wildlife refuge in Alaska to oil and gas drilling, (6) defund efforts to keep raw sewage out of rivers and away from beaches, (7) privatize and open national parks to commercial development, (8) give the few remaining ancient forests over to unrestrained logging, and (9) repeal the Endangered Species Act. In sum, their openly professed intent has been to eviscerate all our environmental protections, however inadequate these are.

Conservatives maintain that there is no environmental crisis. Technological advances will continue to make life better for more and more people.[12] One might wonder why rich and powerful interests take this seemingly suicidal anti-environmental route. They can destroy welfare, public housing, public education, public transportation, social security, Medicare, and Medicaid with impunity, for they and their children will not thereby be deprived, having more than sufficient means to procure private services for themselves. But the environment is a different story. Wealthy conservatives and their corporate lobbyists inhabit the same polluted planet as everyone else, eat the same chemicalized food, and breathe the same toxified air.

In fact, they do not live exactly as everyone else. They experience a different class reality, residing in places where the air is somewhat better than in low and middle income areas. They have access to food that is organically raised and specially prepared. The nation's toxic dumps and freeways usually are not situated in or near their swanky neighborhoods. The pesticide sprays are not poured over their trees and gardens. Clearcutting does not desolate their ranches, estates, and vacation spots. Even when they or their children succumb to a dread

---

[12] A cover story in *Forbes* (8/14/95) derides the "health scare industry" and reassures readers that highly chemicalized and fat-ridden junk foods are perfectly safe for one's health. The magazine's owners and corporate advertisers are aware that if people begin to question the products offered by the corporate system, they may end up questioning the system itself. Not without good cause does *Forbes* describe itself as "a capitalist tool."

disease like cancer, they do not link the tragedy to environmental factors—though scientists now believe that most cancers stem from human-made causes. They deny there is a larger problem because they themselves create that problem and owe much of their wealth to it.

But how can they deny the threat of an ecological apocalypse brought on by ozone depletion, global warming, disappearing top soil, and dying oceans? Do the dominant elites want to see life on earth, including their own, destroyed? In the long run they indeed will be victims of their own policies, along with everyone else. However, like us all, they live not in the long run but in the here and now. For the ruling interests, what is at stake is something of more immediate and greater concern than global ecology: It is global capital accumulation. The fate of the biosphere is an abstraction compared to the fate of one's own investments.

Furthermore, pollution pays, while ecology costs. Every dollar a company must spend on environmental protections is one less dollar in earnings. It is more profitable to treat the environment like a septic tank, pouring thousands of new harmful chemicals into the atmosphere each year, dumping raw industrial effluent into the river or bay, turning waterways into open sewers. The longterm benefit of preserving a river that runs alongside a community (where the corporate polluters do not live anyway) does not weigh as heavily as the immediate gain that comes from ecologically costly modes of production.

Solar, wind, and tidal energy systems could help avert ecological disaster, but they would bring disaster to the rich oil cartels. Six of the world's ten top industrial corporations are involved primarily in the production of oil, gasoline, and motor vehicles. Fossil fuel pollution means billions in profits. Ecologically sustainable forms of production threaten those profits.

Immense and imminent gain for oneself is a far more compelling consideration than a diffuse loss shared by the general public. The cost of turning a forest into a wasteland weighs little against the profits that come from harvesting the timber.

This conflict between immediate private gain on the one hand and remote public benefit on the other operates even at the individual consumer level. Thus, it is in one's longterm interest not to operate a motor vehicle, which contributes more to environmental devastation than any other single consumer item. But we have an immediate need for transportation in order to get to work, or do whatever else needs doing, so most of us have no choice except to own and use automobiles.

The "car culture" demonstrates how the ecological crisis is not primarily an individual matter of man soiling his own nest. In most instances, the "choice" of using a car is no choice at all. Ecologically efficient and less costly electric-car mass transportation has been deliberately destroyed since the 1930s in campaigns waged across the country by the automotive, oil, and tire industries. Corporations involved in transportation put "America on wheels," in order to maximize consumption costs for the public and profits for themselves, and to hell with the environment or anything else.

The enormous interests of giant multinational corporations outweigh doomsayer predictions about an ecological crisis. Sober business heads refuse to get caught up in the "hysteria" about the environment, preferring to quietly augment their fortunes. Besides, there can always be found a few experts who will go against all the evidence and say that the jury is still out, that there is no conclusive proof to support the alarmists. Conclusive proof in this case would come only when we reach the point of no return.

Ecology is profoundly subversive of capitalism. It needs planned, environmentally sustainable production rather than the rapacious unregulated kind. It requires economical consumption rather than an artificially stimulated, ever-expanding consumerism. It calls for natural, low-cost energy systems rather than profitable, high-cost, polluting ones. Ecology's implications for capitalism are too horrendous for the capitalist to contemplate.

Those in the higher circles, who once hired Blackshirts to destroy democracy out of fear that their class interests were threatened, have no trouble doing the same against "eco-terrorists." Those who have waged merciless war against the Reds have no trouble making war against the Greens. Those who have brought us poverty wages, exploitation, unemployment, homelessness, urban decay, and other oppressive economic conditions are not too troubled about bringing us ecological crisis. The plutocrats are more wedded to their wealth than to the Earth upon which they live, more concerned with the fate of their fortunes than with the fate of the planet.[13]

The struggle over environmentalism is part of the class struggle itself, a fact that seems to have escaped many environmentalists. The impending eco-apocalypse is a class act. It has been created by and for the benefit of the few, at the expense of the many. The trouble is, this time the class act may take all of us down, once and forever.

In the relationship between wealth and power, what is at stake is not only economic justice, but democracy itself and the survival of the biosphere. Unfortunately, the struggle for democracy and eco-logical sanity is not likely to be advanced by trendy, jargonized, ABC theorists who treat class as an outmoded concept and who seem ready to consider anything but the realities of capitalist power. In this they are little different from the dominant ideology they profess to oppose. They are the ones who need to get back on this planet.

The only countervailing force that might eventually turn things in a better direction is an informed and mobilized citizenry. Whatever their shortcomings, the people are our best hope. Indeed, we are they. Whether or not the ruling circles still wear blackshirts, and whether or not their opponents are Reds, *la lutta continua*, the strug-gle continues, today, tomorrow, and through all history.

---

[13] In June 1996, speaking at a U.N. conference in Istanbul, Turkey, Fidel Castro noted: "Those who have almost destroyed the planet and poisoned the air, the seas, the rivers and the earth are those who are least interested in saving humanity."

Index

ABOUT THE AUTHOR

MICHAEL PARENTI is considered one of the nation's leading progressive thinkers. He received his Ph.D. in political science from Yale University in 1962, and has taught at a number of colleges and universities. His writings have been featured in scholarly journals, popular periodicals, and newspapers, and have been translated into Spanish, Chinese, Polish, Portuguese, Japanese, and Turkish.

Dr. Parenti lectures around the country on college campuses and before religious, labor, community, peace, and public interest groups. He has appeared on radio and television talk shows to discuss current issues or ideas from his published works. Tapes of his talks have played on numerous radio stations to enthusiastic audiences. Audio and video tapes of his talks are sold on a not-for-profit basis; for a listing, contact People's Video, P.O. Box 99514, Seattle WA 98199; tel. 206 789-5371. Dr. Parenti lives in Berkeley, California.